THE ONLY LAND I KNOW

THE
Iroquois
AND THEIR
NEIGHBORS

Laurence M. Hauptman, *Series Editor*

Although officially designated the *Lumber River*, those who love her prefer the more melodious name of *Lumbee*. As the poet John Charles McNeill said in the early twentieth century, "She is a tortuous, delicious flirt, but she does not deserve the punishment put upon her by geographers, who have perverted her sweet Indian name of 'Lumbee' into something that suggests choking sawdust, rotting slabs and the shrill screams of the circular saw."

—Photo by William P. Revels

THE ONLY LAND I KNOW

A HISTORY OF THE LUMBEE INDIANS

ADOLPH L. DIAL
DAVID K. ELIADES

SYRACUSE UNIVERSITY PRESS

First Syracuse University Press Edition 1996
96 97 98 99 00   6 5 4 3 2 1

This book was originally published in 1975 by the Indian Historian Press, Inc., San Francisco.

The paper used in this publication meets the minimum requirements of American National Standard for Information Sciences—Permanence of Paper for Printed Library Materials, ANSI Z39.48-1984. ∞™

Library of Congress Cataloging-in-Publication Data
Dial, Adolph L., 1922–
The only land I know : a history of the Lumbee Indians / Adolph L. Dial, David K. Eliades.
p.   cm. — (The Iroquois and their neighbors)
Originally published: San Francisco : Indian Historian Press, c1975
Includes bibliographical references.
ISBN 0-8156-0360-6 (pbk. : alk. paper)
1. Lumbee Indians—History. I.–Eliades, David K., 1938– .
II. Title. III. Series.
E99.C91D52—1995
975.6′1004975—dc20   95-31949

Manufactured in the United States of America

For Mary Doris and Darby—
may their world be one of love and understanding.

ADOLPH L. DIAL, now professor emeritus, was a longtime member of the faculty of Pembroke State University. During his academic career, he served as chair of the Department of History and Political Science, was instrumental in the establishment of the Department of American Indian Studies and served as its first chair, published widely on Lumbee history, and received two honorary doctorates for his achievements and contributions. Additionally, he has been a successful businessman and civic leader, including service in the North Carolina House of Representatives. He has also been involved in the ongoing effort of his people to gain full federal recognition as the Lumbee Tribe of Cheraw Indians. For his many accomplishments, he was awarded the Henry Berry Lowry Award, the highest honor bestowed by the Lumbee community.

DAVID K. ELIADES is professor and chair of the Department of History at Pembroke State University. His areas of specialization are white-Indian relations in the colonial Carolinas, American military history, and state-local history—areas in which he has numerous publications. He is a member of "The National Faculty," which works to strengthen public education; he has been named an Outstanding Teacher on four different occasions; and he was named the first Distinguished Professor in the history of Pembroke State University.

Contents

Illustrations

Preface

This book is essentially a narrative of the major personalities, experiences, hopes, and fears of the Lumbee Indians of southeastern North Carolina. Writing the history of a people is complex, even frustrating, but a satisfyng process just the same. History is, after all, the drama of life itself. The people, their problems, and their achievements in the face of great adversity are real, not products of one's imagination. In reliving the past, one cannot help but better understand and appreciate the present.

From necessity, parts of this book are based on logical supposition and oral history. The Lumbees, like other Indians, have never been great keepers of written records, but they do have a strong oral tradition. While it is fashionable among some historians to attack oral history as inherently imprecise and largely inaccurate, yet they willingly use memoirs written years after the fact, or documents that have been intentionally or unintentionally edited. Where's the justice? The objective of any historical study is, idealistically, truth. Should not all sources be explored and utilized in pursuit of this goal? Moreover, it is well to remember that history is not a precise science. Realistically, history is both what existed and what historians through research come to believe existed. There are always pieces missing from the historical puzzle, and an absolute reconstruction of the past is not possible.

Since no general history of the Lumbee Indians has been previously written, this book, by its very nature, is a pioneering effort. The authors expect and hope that future historians will improve and enlarge upon their findings. More importantly, all the time and effort which went into this project was well spent if the ultimate results are a broadening of knowledge and an increased capacity for understanding on the part of the readers.

The scholarly debts one incurs while writing a book are numerous and heavy. It is impossible to thank individually all the people and institutions that have assisted us over the past four years. But we do wish to thank The Ford Foundation for a generous research grant, and the Lumbee people collectively. Without their cooperation this book could never have been written.

Finally, we also want to thank our wives, Ruth Jones Dial and Celene Rozier Eliades, for their patience and support. Celene Eliades deserves special commendation for typing the manuscript through its many revisions.

Adolph L. Dial
David K. Eliades
November 1, 1974

Introduction

The Lumbee River is an old stream that seems to wander aim-
lessly as it carves its snake-like pattern in the terrain of southeastern North Carolina.[1] At some places the river's darkness reaches
down into the earth only several feet. Then, a distance of yards
downstream, it gashes the earth as if angry and determined to
show its power. It begins forebodingly as Drowning Creek, a
name it has earned many times over, draws strength from tributaries as it maneuvers eastward; then, almost imperceptibly, it
blends with other waters to become the Pee Dee River, emptying
finally in the Atlantic Ocean off the coast of South Carolina.

For most of its length, the Lumbee flows through swamps and
woodlands, a shadowy world of half-seen creatures and movements, a world in which man has intruded, where nature can
never be forgotten. Fittingly in 1953, this brooding mercurial river
gave its name to the largest body of Indians in the Eastern United
States.[2]

Like the river, the Lumbee Indians have mystery, excitement,
and violence in their history; and like the river, they persevere.

1. While the river is now officially designated as the Lumber River, it has been known col-
loquially as the Lumbee for many years, particularly among the Indian people.
2. In the past, the Lumbees have been known variously as the Croatan Indians, the Indians
of Robeson County, and the Cherokee Indians of Robeson County.

Who are the Lumbee Indians? They are approximately 40,000 people living mainly in Robeson and adjoining counties in southeastern North Carolina, with colonies in several of the nation's largest cities. They are a people in which the Indian strain is very strong. Yet, they so thoroughly adopted the white man's lifestyle several centuries ago that they can point to no extensive remaining Indian culture. They are a proud people who have their own central community of Pembroke, North Carolina, who own land and excel as farmers, established their own churches, schools and businesses. They have never been placed on reservations, nor have they been wards of either the state or the federal government. They are a people who have fought, and still are willing to fight for their rights.

However, to examine the Lumbees in terms of "minority" or material status illustrates only their situation as it is today. The question remains: "Who are the Lumbee Indians? What are their origins?" While the question itself is simple, the answer is complex and clouded in mystery. To be a Lumbee is to be cloaked in the myths and uncertainties of the past, to find your pride in Indianness being challenged and denigrated. Most important, it is to find some of one's basic rights as an American and a human being restricted if not denied. Indeed, shorn of all frills, the history of the Lumbees is a history of struggle. The total story is one of struggle to gain acceptance as Indians, to escape the emasculating effects of discriminatory laws and to join the mainstream of society as first-class citizens. The Lumbees, by whatever name they were variously called through the centuries, have always known themselves as Indians. They have been known, recognized, and mistreated as Indians by their surrounding white communities. Theirs has been a centuries-old struggle indeed. But while the struggle is certainly not over, the Indian people are meeting the challenges they face, with considerable success.

THE ONLY LAND I KNOW

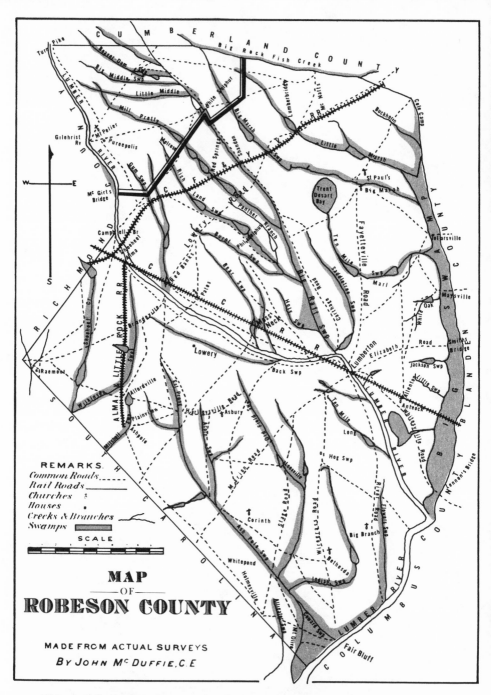

MAP
—OF—
ROBESON COUNTY

MADE FROM ACTUAL SURVEYS
BY JOHN McDUFFIE, C.E.

This map shows the many swamps that existed in Robeson County. The importance of this geographical feature is that the swamps provided the Lumbee Indians isolation, protection, and fertile lands, in the past. The nature of the locality influenced their history. The town of Pembroke, the central community of the Lumbees, is not found on the map because it was not established until later. Using this map for reference, Pembroke is located about half way between the communities of Pates and Moss Neck on the railroad line running from the southeast to the northwest.

—Map courtesy of THE ROBESONIAN

1

A People of Traditions

When Scottish immigrants began to settle the upper reaches of North Carolina's Cape Fear Valley in the early 1730's, they were amazed to find a group of English-speaking people already living near the Lumbee River. Far from being the "savages" no doubt expected by the Scots, these Indians lived in simple houses, farmed in the European manner, and generally practiced many of the arts of European life. The Scots had found the ancestors of the Lumbee Indians. How the Lumbees came to live in such a geographically inaccessible area, in the manner they did, has long been the subject of historical speculation.

Clinging fiercely to their Indian origins, the Lumbees nonetheless have no remnants of their Indian language which might provide clues to their relationships with other Native Americans. Only traditions and folktales remain as evidence, tales which link this unique group with the lost survivors of the Roanoke Colony as well as with the Eastern band of the Sioux Indians, the powerful and highly assimilated Cherokee, and the Tuscarora Indians. Each tradition has its supporters; each has its detractors. But each is worth examining for the clues it offers about the origins of the remarkable Lumbee Indians.

In 1584, Sir Walter Raleigh obtained a charter from Queen Elizabeth I giving him the right to possess lands in the New World not already under Christian control. Raleigh promptly sent explorers to determine the nature of the lands within his grant, and to find a site suitable for a colony. The explorers examined the coastal region of North Carolina, which they named *Virginia* in honor of the unmarried queen, and returned with a glowing account of Roanoke Island and the surrounding area. As a result, a colonizing effort was made on Roanoke Island in 1585-1586; this attempt was abortive. Beset by internal dissension, supply shortages, and Indian hostilities, the colonists returned to England. Ironically, within a month after their departure, three ships reached the Roanoke area with needed supplies and additional colonists. Finding all settlers gone, fifteen courageous men were now left on Roanoke Island to maintain England's claim to the region.

THE LUMBEE INDIANS AND THE LOST COLONY

Although Raleigh was disappointed over the failure of his initial colonizing effort, he was nevertheless determined to establish a permanent English "nation" in America, and so, in 1587, he sent a second colony of 117 men, women, and children to the New World, under Governor John White. This group was instructed not to settle on Roanoke Island, largely because of those Indians in the area who were angered by earlier mistreatment, and had become suspicious of the Englishmen's intentions. It should be noted, however, that most Indians in the vicinity remained well-disposed toward settlers. White was told to stop at the island and see if the fifteen men left there in 1586 were still alive. While none of the fifteen could be found, the visit proved to be of momentous importance. For unknown reasons and contrary to its instructions, the White expedition remained at Roanoke Island, thus precipitating a fascinating sequence of historic events.

The John White Colony reached the New World in midsummer, too late to plant and harvest a crop. The settlers quickly realized they had inadequate supplies to carry them through the coming winter and they urged Governor White to return to England for new supplies. Although reluctant to leave, White finally consented, and sailed for home in late August, 1587. Upon reaching England, John White found the mother country to be at war with Spain. The war was essentially an outgrowth of economic and religious rivalries: King Philip II of Spain, frustrated in his many attempts to bring England under Spanish control, was now so determined to destroy his Protestant rival that he ordered the construction of the "invincible Armada," a fleet of 130 ships which imperiled the freedom and independence of England. Although the English, through a combination of fast ships, boldness, discipline, and good fortune, defeated the Armada in the summer of 1588, Spain remained a formidable seapower. Thus, White could not safely embark for America until 1590, reaching Roanoke Island in August of that year. The Governor had been gone for three years. When he finally landed on the island and sought the settlers, there were none to be found. The colony had disappeared, becoming known to history as "The Lost Colony." Somewhat surprisingly, most historians share the judgment of a noted North Carolina scholar, Samuel A'Court Ashe, who wrote: "When the colonists receded from White's view, as he left the shores of Virginia, they passed from the domain of history, and all we know is that misfortune and distress overtook them; and that they miserably perished, their sad fate being one of those deplorable sacrifices that have always attended the accomplishment of great human purposes." It is incredible that historians so naively accept this assumption that the colonists died of starvation, disease, and Indian hostilities, and blithely disregard evidence to the contrary.

Governor John White, based on his written account, was not unduly concerned over his failure to find the settlers. He noted that the possibility of the colony moving inland for fifty miles had been discussed prior to his departure for England. It had been agreed that if such a move were made, the settlers would so indicate with a marking. It was also agreed that if they were in danger when they left, they would signify this with a cross. While locating no inhabitants on Roanoke Island, White did find, carved on a tree, the letters "C.R.O." and on a gatepost the word "CROATOAN." Significantly, there was no cross indicating distress. Moreover, most of the goods left behind were possessions of the Governor, or goods which would have been burdensome on a long journey. In addition, most articles had been buried as if the settlers hoped to return and recover them at some future date.

John White wrote, concerning his discoveries: ". . . I greatly joyed that I had safely found a certain token of their being at Croatoan, which is the place where Manteo was born, and the savages of the island our friend." Though White sought the missing settlers, bad weather and the desire of the sailing master to move on to the West Indies resulted in a perfunctory search and revealed nothing. The important point is that White was confident the settlers were alive and that they had gone to live with the Hatteras Tribe of the trustworthy Manteo, whose friendship dated back to the discovery of Roanoke Island in 1584. The fact that the colonists were not seen again does not prove they perished, or ceased to have a role in history.

The fate of the John White Colony continued to be of concern to Walter Raleigh and other Englishmen for years to come. Raleigh urged every ship sailing to the vicinity of North Carolina to seek news concerning the lost colonists, though none ever returned with useful information. Then, with the successful establishment of a colony at Jamestown in 1607, two Englishmen of that colony attempted to discover what had become of the missing settlers. Captain John Smith records in his *True Relation*, written in 1608, that information obtained from Indians in the Jamestown vicinity told about men in the Chowan-Roanoke River area of North Carolina who dressed like Englishmen. William Strachey, secretary of Virginia Colony wrote, supposedly in 1613, *A Historie of Travaile into Virginia Britannia;* he cites reports of Indians that White's colonists did indeed move inland where they constructed two-story stone houses and lived with the Indians for twenty years. This peaceful existence ended with the coming of the Jamestown settlement. The further incursion of Englishmen excited and angered the "priests" who were advisors of the great chief Powhatan and who, according to Strachey, convinced that powerful leader to order the slaughter of the survivors of the missing colony. Strachey reports that some escaped, but none ever had communication with Jamestown. There are several problems with accepting Strachey's account. To begin with, it is not at all certain, and indeed doubtful, that Powhatan controlled the area where the surviving colonists were to be found.

Moreover, it strains logic to accept that a small band of whites, intermixed with Indians, could have been the objects of such hatred as Strachey describes. Logic indicates that the Indians would have turned on the Jamestown settlers, rather than upon those far removed in North Carolina. In addition, Indian societies were extraordinarily tolerant toward people who willingly joined with them, and there's little reason to believe that this wasn't the case concerning the colonists from Roanoke Island.

ENGLISH-SPEAKING INDIANS

In the mid-seventeenth century, two more adventurous individuals braved the hazards of travel into little-known regions and reported their findings. The first was the Reverend Morgan Jones, who claimed to have marched to North Carolina from Port Royal, South Carolina, in 1660, and to have been captured and then befriended by Indians who spoke English. His descriptions indicate the possibility of his having been in the area of Robeson County, the central location of the Lumbees. Though Jones makes no mention of the "Lost Colony," nor of his captors having a European culture, the fact of his having found natives who spoke English certainly indicates outside influence. Unfortunately, the reliability of Jones' letter is questionable in that it was not written until 1686 and the only extant copy is a newspaper record of the letter, published in the *Gentlemen's Gazette* in 1840.

The second adventurer who traveled through parts of North Carolina in the seventeenth century was John Lederer, a German who began his expedition in Virginia on May 20, 1670, and ended it back in that colony on July 18, 1670. If the information contained in Lederer's account is accurate, it appears that he entered the state at a north-central location (Warren County, N. C.), traveled eastward toward the Roanoke River area, proceeded southwestward through the vicinity of Robeson County, and then crossed into South Carolina. The route of his march has been ascertained both by geographical features he noted and by Indian tribes with which he came into contact. He claimed to have visited, among major tribes, the Chowanoc, Tuscarora,

Cheraw, and Santee Indians; the first two were in North Carolina and the latter two in South Carolina. The great difficulty with Lederer's information is that two months for such a journey through largely wilderness conditions seems too brief a span of time. It is quite possible that some of Lederer's material is factual, and other information hearsay. At any rate, the most important statement he made concerning the possible fate of the "Lost Colony" came when he was in the border area of the Carolinas. Lederer wrote of his visit: "Here I made a day's stay to inform myself further in these countries; and understood both from the Usheries (Santee) and some Sara (Cheraw) Indians that come to trade with them, that two days' journey and a half from hence to the southwest, a powerful nation of bearded men were seated, which I suppose to be the Spaniards, because the Indians never have any, it being a universal custom among them to prevent their growth by plucking the young hair out by the roots." While it is possible that the bearded men were Spaniards, or that they were Englishmen from a Barbadian colony on the lower Cape Fear River, it is also possible that they were English survivors of the "Lost Colony" intermixed with Indians and removed inland from the coast.

In 1709, John Lawson, surveyor-general of North Carolina and a long-time friend of the Indians in the colony, published his *History of Carolina*. This work recounted Lawson's journey from Charleston, South Carolina, northward to the Neuse River area of North Carolina. Lawson was an observant and perceptive traveler, and his record of what he did and saw constitutes one of the best sources modern historians have on the geography and peoples of the areas of the Carolinas as yet not settled by Europeans. Indeed, Lawson's account is so reliable that he has been labeled the "first North Carolina historian."

Lawson's journal indicates that he traveled up the Santee and Wateree Rivers, across the foothills of the Carolinas to the headwaters of the tributaries of the Neuse, and then down those rivers to the coast. He apparently passed through the country of the Catawbas, the Tuscaroras, and the Corees. Interestingly, Lawson notes that as he approached the coast of North Carolina he was given two chickens by friendly Indians—a clear indication of contact with Europeans because the eastern Indians of North America had no domestic fowl prior to the coming of the whites. During his travels, Lawson gained the services of an Indian guide named Enoe-Will, a man "always ready to serve the English, not out of gain, but real affection." Based on accounts of his youth, related by Enoe-Will, Lawson deduced that he was a Coree Indian. One night after making camp, Lawson pulled out a copy of an illustrated Bible which the guide asked to see. Lawson granted the guide's request, and then asked Will if he did not wish to become a Chrisian; the Indian sharply declined. However, he stated his willingness to have Lawson take his son and educate him in the ways of the whites. Lawson's comments make it clear that Enoe-Will was familiar with the ability of the English to "talk in a book" and to "make paper speak" (read and write). It is conjectured that the Coree Indians perhaps came into contact with Englishmen, possibly survivors of the "Lost Colony," prior to or during Enoe-Will's boyhood.

Further evidence of early English influence among some of the coastal Indians of North Carolina is given by Lawson in a part of his book entitled "*A Description of North-Carolina.*" In this part, Lawson wrote of Raleigh's missing colony; he said:

> A farther Confirmation of this we have from the Hatteras Indians, who either then lived on Roanoak-Island, or much frequented it. These tell us, that several of their Ancestors were white People, and could talk in a Book, as we do; the Truth of which is confirm'd by gray Eyes being found frequently amongst these Indians, and no others. They value themselves extremely for their Affinity to the English, and are ready to do them all friendly Offices. It is probable, that this Settlement miscarry'd for want of timely Supplies from England; or thro' the Treachery of the Natives, for we may reasonably suppose that the English were forced to cohabit with them, for Relief and Conversation; and that in process of Time, they conform'd themselves to the Manners of their Indian Relations.

The sum total of these statements is that at least some of the missing Raleigh colonists survived, and intermingled with friendly

Indians. There is no other conclusion that can withstand close scrutiny. What became of the survivors cannot be ascertained from the comments of these early observers, but fortunately there is other evidence.

"LOST COLONY" SURVIVORS

In 1888, Hamilton MacMillan, one of the best white friends the Indians of Robeson County ever had, an able state legislator and local historian, published a pamphlet entitled "Sir Walter Raleigh's Lost Colony: A Historical Sketch of the Attempts of Sir Walter Raleigh to Establish a Colony in Virginia, with the Traditions of an Indian Tribe in North Carolina, Indicating the Fate of the Colony of Englishmen Left on Roanoke Island in 1587." In this work MacMillan vigorously defended the tradition that at least some of the Raleigh colonists survived and joined with Manteo's tribe migrating ultimately to Robeson County. MacMillan so strongly believed this, that, the year prior to publishing his pamphlet he succeeded in getting the North Carolina General Assembly to designate the Indians of Robeson County as the *Croatan Indians,* erroneously believing this to be the name of the tribe with which the colonists took refuge.[1]

MacMillan's position was supported by a prominent lawyer and businessman in Robeson named Angus Wilton McLean, who became a governor of North Carolina in the 1920's. Although McLean believed strongly that there was Cherokee blood among people in the area, he definitely accepted the Lumbee tradition of "Lost Colony" descent. McLean wrote, in a letter to the Commissioner of Indian Affairs in 1914; "My opinion is, from a very exhaustive examination. . . that these Indians are not only descendants of Sir Walter Raleigh's lost colony. . . but that they are also mixed with the Cherokee Indians." This future governor went on to say that the Lumbees "from time immemorial" have contended that they were "of Cherokee descent and they further have

1. As noted earlier in the text, Croatan was a place occupied by Hatteras Indians and MacMillan should have sought recognition for the people as descendants of that historic tribe.

a tradition among them that their ancestors, or some of them, came from 'Roanoke and Virginia.' Roanoke and Virginia, of course, originally comprised all of eastern North Carolina, including Roanoke Island, the settlement of Sir Walter Raleigh's lost colony." The relationship of the Cherokee and Lumbee people will be examined shortly, but the important point is that Mc-Lean, a learned and competent man, was convinced and had long heard that the Lumbees could trace their familes back to the missing Raleigh Colony.

Stephen B. Weeks, a professional historian with a national reputation, was also a strong proponent of the "Lost Colony" thesis. In 1891, Weeks published, in the *Papers of the American Historical Association,* an article entitled "The Lost Colony of Roanoke: Its fate and survival." After examining the evidence, oral and written, Professor Weeks concluded: "The Croatans (Lumbees) of to-day claim descent from the lost colony. Their habits, disposition, and mental characteristics show traces of Indian and European ancestry. Their language is the English of three hundred years ago, and their names are in many cases the same as those borne by the original colonists. No other theory of their origin has been advanced, and it is confidently believed that the one here proposed is logically and historically the best, supported as it is both by external and internal evidence. If this theory is rejected, then the critic must explain in some other way the origin of a people which, after the lapse of three hundred years, show the characteristics, speak the language, and possess the family names of the second English colony planted in the western world."

In 1914, the United States Senate adopted a resolution authorizing the Secretary of the Interior "to cause an investigation to be made of the condition and tribal rights of the Indians of Robeson and Adjoining counties of North Carolina. . ." To carry out this investigation, Special Indian Agent O. M. McPherson was sent to Robeson County. Through numerous interviews, examination of pertinent literature, and historical research, McPherson produced an extensive and thorough report both on the history and existing condition of the Lumbees. In the course of his investigation, McPherson confronted the question of the relationship of the Lumbees to Raleigh's Lost Colony. The agent wrote:

"There is a tradition among these people at the present time that their ancestors were the lost colony, amalgamated with some tribe of Indians. This tradition is supported by their looks, their complexion, color of skin, hair and eyes, by their manners, customs and habits, and by the fact that while they are, in part, of undoubted Indian origin, they have no Indian names and no Indian language. . ." When his investigation was complete, McPherson was convinced of the validity of the Lumbee claim of descent from the "Lost Colony."

But what is the specific evidence on which these prominent men and scholars rest their case? Generally, they were all convinced that the colonists were not really lost—that they simply moved to the mainland to live with friendly Indians, thus tying their future to that of their native brothers. In other words, they accepted the testimony of John White, John Smith, William Strachey and others. The failure of early adventurers to make direct contact with the survivors did not distress them, because they realized that *Croatoan,* to which the settlers indicated they removed, was not a clearly defined location; some accounts and maps indicate that it was an island to the south of Roanoke, while other sources indicate that it was a part of the mainland. In fact, no one knew exactly where the settlers went. It is quite possible that the word "Croatoan" meant more than one particular place. "Croatoan" might have been the designation for a hunting area to the Hatteras people, a designation the white settlers would not necessarily have understood. Consequently, finding Croatoan might not have been as simple as even John White had supposed.

THE RECORDS OF HISTORY

All these scholars were impressed by the names found among the Lumbees, clearly similar to some of those listed on the John White log. There were one hundred and seventeen settlers still on Roanoke Island when the governor sailed back to England for additional supplies in 1587. Among those settlers there were ninety-five different surnames. As counted by Hamilton Mac-Millan, forty-one of these surnames (more than forty-three percent), including such names as Dare, Cooper, Stevens, Sampson, Harvie, Howe, Cage, Cheven, Jones, Brooks, and others, were found among the Lumbees, a people living more than two hundred miles away from Roanoke Island. Even more remarkable, as MacMillan found in the late nineteenth century and as is occasionally found among some of the older residents today, was the fact that "the traditions of every family bearing the name of one of the lost colonists point to Roanoke Island as the home of their ancestors." While some of the family names that existed earlier have disappeared, the comparison of names is still striking. Admittedly, most of these names are fairly common English names, and the similarity of names would not in itself prove a connection with the "Lost Colony." But this development, added to the fact that there is no other satisfactory explanation as to why the Indians of Robeson County have English names, must be considered as additional evidence in explaining what happened to Raleigh's colonists and identifying the origin of the Lumbees.

Moreover, the Lumbees, prior to the breakdown of their geographical isolation in the mid-twentieth century with the advent of mass media, spoke a pure Old English. Their language differed from that of the whites and blacks among whom they lived. According to Dr. Stephen Weeks, "They have preserved many forms in good use three hundred years ago, but which are now obsolete in the written language and are found only in colloquial and dialectical English." He went on to describe how the Lumbees drawled the final syllable in every sentence and how they began all greetings with "mon-n-n," which meant *man*. Weeks, as well as other observers, also noted that they usually began their traditions with the phrase: "Mon, my fayther told me that his fayther told him," and so forth. To further illustrate the old English patterns and characteristics of their speech, Weeks wrote:

They retain the parasitic (glide) y, which was an extremely common development in Anglo-Saxon, in certain words through the palatal influence of the previous consonant, pronouncing cow as cy-ow, cart as cy-art, card as cy-ard, girl as gy-irl, kind as ky-ind... The dialectical Jeams is found in place of James. They regularly use mon for man; mension for measurement; aks for ask; hit for it; hosen for hose; housen for houses; crone is to push down and wit means knowledge.

One is reminded that these speech characteristics were present when the first whites came into contact with the Lumbees in the early eighteenth century and that they persisted to a considerable extent until the 1950's. More important, no one has yet offered an alternative explanation as to how these people learned to speak that type of English and made it their natural language, if they were not influenced by settlers from Raleigh's missing colony.

Still, all the evidence offered to this point does not satisfy the skeptics. Samuel Ashe, a writer determined to preserve the purity and romance of the "Lost Colony," even in defiance of logic, and evidence to the contrary, wrote concerning the Lumbees: "Because names borne by some of the colonists have been found among a mixed race in Robeson County, now called Croatans (Lumbees), an inference has been drawn that there was some connection between them. It is highly improbable that English names would have been preserved among a tribe of savages beyond the second generation, there being no communication except with other savages." In other words, most scholars invariably argue that if the Raleigh colonists went to live with Manteo and his people, they would, in due course, have adopted the Indian's culture, rather than the reverse occurring. This is particularly interesting, because virtually no one seems to have considered the demography of the situation. Many Indian villages consisted of as few as ten to fifteen families, and this was quite possibly the case with Manteo's village. If so, and this is more logical than assuming that there were hundreds of Hatteras people living at Croatan then it is indeed conceivable that the English culture predominated and the Indians were assimilated by the whites. Even the skeptics are unable to explain how the Lumbees came to have their distinctively English culture. Moreover, even Ashe, noted for his white supremacist attitudes in the late nineteenth century, admitted that ". . . many persons believed them to be the descendants of the Lost Colony; and the Legislature has officially designated them an 'Croatans;' and has treated them as Indians."

It is also important to note that there are traditions among the

12

Lumbees that their ancestors moved from their former coastal homes to the Black River area of North Carolina in the vicinity of present-day Sampson County. The time of their removal from the Black River region to the banks of the Lumbee River is uncertain, but all the traditions of the people point to a time prior to the Tuscarora War, and it seems likely that they were settled in Robeson County as early as 1650. All of this, though based on oral history, again seems logical, for Indians were a mobile people and certainly the whites who had joined them would have wanted to avoid conflict with any hostile people. The fact of their difference would have made this mixed group wary of other peoples, particularly if the white culture prevailed, as seems likely. Understandably, they would have moved into a largely unsettled area and continued to seek a location which would guarantee them the most isolation. Robeson County would have been viewed as the "promised land" for a people seeking to escape contact, because this county was virtually surrounded by swamps for centuries, with only a few trails cut through it. It was one of the last areas settled by whites, and one of the least desirable locations from the standpoint of most Indians. A people who sought isolation would certainly find it in Robeson, and they did. In short, geography seems to be the real explanation as to why the Lumbees retained the English language and mode of living, their legacy from the "Lost Colony."

While proof of Lumbee descent from the Lost Colony, in the form of birth records and other documents is most unlikely to be found, the circumstantial evidence, when joined with logic, unquestionably supports the Lumbee tradition that there was a real and lasting connection with the Raleigh Settlement. The survival of colonists' names, the uniqueness of the Lumbee dialect in the past, the oral traditions, the demography of sixteenth century North Carolina, the mobility of the Indian people, human adaptability and the isolation of Robeson County, all prove the "Lost Colony" theory. When one combines these factors with the determination of men to survive regardless of the century in which they live, and the fact that no one can satisfactorily explain the English culture of the Lumbees—a culture obviously adopted over a long period of time, for all traces of Indian culture could not have been obliterated in one or even two generations—no other conclusion is reasonable.

THE LUMBEE INDIANS AND THE CHEROKEE

Because the white population of southeastern North Carolina turned the name *Croatoan* into a label of disdain and even derision, the Indian people sought a name with no derogatory connotations. Because of a tradition, dating back to the early eighteenth century, that there was considerable Cherokee blood in the Indian community, the State Legislature designated the people in 1913 as the *Cherokee Indians of Robeson County*. The people carried this name until 1953.

The basis for the claim of Cherokee blood is found in the Tuscarora War of 1711-1713. In what was the bloodiest Indian war in North Carolina's history, the Tuscaroras rose up to avenge the loss of lands, cheating traders, and the practice of Indian slavery. The threat to the colony was so serious that Governor Edward Hyde promptly asked for aid from Virginia and South Carolina. While Virginia offered help under conditions which North Carolina found unacceptable, South Carolina quickly responded with a force of whites and friendly Indians under Colonel John ("Tuscarora Jack") Barnwell. Although Barnwell was unable to break the power of the Tuscaroras, he did force them to sign a truce. Unhappily for Barnwell, who had been wounded in the fighting and had incurred considerable expenses, the North Carolinians were ungrateful; they wanted the Tuscaroras destroyed as a threat to the colony. Consequently, when Barnwell appeared before the North Carolina Assembly requesting financial compensation and a reward of land for his efforts, his requests were denied. The assembly took the position that he had not ended the danger to the colony and thus was not entitled to money or land. Angrily, Barnwell left North Carolina. As he and his army departed, some Tuscaroras were seized to be sold as slaves. The departure of the South Carolinians and their seizure of the Tuscaroras led to a renewal of the conflict. The power of the Tuscaroras was not finally destroyed until 1713 when Colonel James Moore, aided by his brother Maurice, defeated the Indians at their stronghold of Fort Nohoroco.

The Barnwell expedition is particularly significant, because tradition has it that this force marched through Robeson County on its way home from the fighting. Moreover, several historians and ethnologists reported that Barnwell's army included a number of Cherokee warriors. Lumbee tradition says that some of the Cherokees with Barnwell chose to stay in Robeson County, after they had participated with whites in the war against the Tuscaroras. It is further related that once they had decided to stay in Robeson they abandoned their Indian culture and mixed with the local population. This theory was advocated by Angus Wilton McLean, who, as noted, later became governor of the state, and certainly the General Assembly of North Carolina was influenced through a belief in the probability of this tradition.

There are, however, several obstacles to accepting the Cherokee theory. Barnwell, in a report dated 1712, mentions no Cherokees in his army, though he did name a number of other tribes. It is doubtful then, that "several hundred" Cherokees fought with Barnwell, as some sources claim, or he would almost surely have mentioned them as a part of his force. More likely, there were a few individual Cherokees who took part as members of both the Barnwell and Moore expeditions, men who were perhaps involved in trade with the backcountry, or mixed Cherokees, the offspring of white trader fathers and Cherokee mothers. In addition, it is difficult to explain how the Cherokees, mountain people and bitter enemies of the Catawbas and their kinsmen, could have allied with them against the Tuscaroras. In short, it is possible that a few Cherokees did fight in the Tuscarora War and did remain in Robeson County, but these Indians were most certainly few in number and had already been largely assimilated into the white culture when this happened. All aspects of Cherokee culture would not have disappeared by the 1730's, when the Scots began to arrive, and there is no evidence indicating that these first European settlers found anything but an English culture. Indeed, it is far more likely that some Lumbees went west with the Cherokees who passed through the area, established a lasting relationship with them, and then that some of their descendants returned to Robeson County in later years.

The oral tradition of Cherokee blood is so strong among the Lumbees, and has been supported so strongly by local historians who conducted extensive investigations, that it is impossible to dismiss the claim. Moreover, it is of considerable interest that a Cherokee chief was George Lowrie, said to be related to some of the Robeson County Lowries. A reasonable assessment of the Cherokee theory leads to the conclusion that some Cherokee blood was introduced into the Lumbee community in the early eighteenth century, but on a small scale. Then, throughout the eighteenth and early nineteenth centuries, frequent contacts between the two peoples led to sporadic intermixing, as the Lumbees sought a stronger Indian connection, while the Cherokees were striving to adapt more thoroughly to the white man's lifestyle, which they accomplished by the 1820's, though it did not save them from removal. Plainly, the Cherokee connection seems definitely to have existed, to have taken place over a considerable span of time, and to have existed between the Lumbees and the more fully assimilated individuals of the Cherokee people.

THE LUMBEE INDIANS AND THE EASTERN SIOUX

The lands now occupied by the Lumbee Indians were once controlled by Indians of the Eastern Siouan linguistic family. How the Eastern Sioux became detached from the main body of Siouan Indians is not known, but they were definitely living a settled existence in the Carolinas by the sixteenth century, because Spanish explorers make reference to them. Generally, these southern Siouan people lived on the banks of rivers, and led sedentary lives, based on agriculture supplemented by hunting and fishing. The most powerful and influential of the Eastern Siouan tribes was the Catawba. Other important members of this family were the Cheraw, Winyah, Keyauwee, Santee, Pee Dee, and Waccamaw. Broadly speaking, the Eastern Sioux, and especially the Catawba, were hereditary enemies of the Cherokee and Tuscarora peoples, though the reasons for this enmity are unknown. One legend explains that the Sioux were late comers to the South and settled on Iroquoian lands, but this has not been verified by archeological evidence.[2] Generally, the Siouan peoples were friendly to the English and usually fought with them against their European and Indian enemies.

Because of Siouan domination of the lands in southeastern North Carolina, the possibility of a connection between these people and the Lumbees has long been recognized. Special Indian Agent O. M. McPherson noted, "It is not improbable. . . that there was some degree of amalgamation between the Indians residing on the Lumbee River and the Cheraws, who were their nearest neighbors." This belief was echoed some years later by Stanley South serving at the time as state archeologist for North Carolina and author of *Indians in North Carolina.* South wrote: "Since this group of Indians [the Lumbees] is located in the area where the Cheraw were living when last heard of, it would not be unreasonable to suggest that they are probably the descendants of this Siouan tribe." The eminent ethnologist, John R. Swanton, though unconvinced that the Lumbees were descended from the "Lost Colony," was more certain that they had a relationship with various bands of the Eastern Sioux peoples. In his book *The Indian Tribes of North America,* he told of the Keyauwee tribe which was first found in Piedmont, North Carolina, but had migrated to the Pee Dee River area by the early eighteenth century, where they joined with the Cheraw and possibly several other lesser tribes. Swanton wrote: "In the Jeffreys atlas of 1761 their town (Keyauwee) appears close to the boundary line between the two Carolinas. They do not reappear in any of the historical records but probably united ultimately in part with the Catawba, while some of their descendants are represented among the Robeson County Indians, often miscalled Croatan." In a portion of his book dealing with the Woccon Indians, Swanton records that the first mention of this tribe was made by John Lawson in 1701 and that he reported the tribe to be quite large, having about 120 warriors.

---

2. Both the Cherokee and Tuscarora Indians were members of the Iroquoian linguistic family.

Swanton then states: "Lack of any earlier mention of such a large tribe lends strength to the theory of Dr. Douglas L. Rights that they were originally Waccamaw. They took part against the Whites in the Tuscarora War and were probably extinguished as a tribe at that time, the remnant fleeing north with the Tuscarora, uniting with the Catawba, or combining with other Siouan remnants in the people later known as Croatan."

THE "LUMBEE" NAME

Partly because of the geographical circumstances which located them in Eastern Sioux territory, partly because some of the people wanted a more precise identity than they then had, and partly because the federal government was sympathetic to the condition of the American Indian during Franklin Roosevelt's first administrations, a number of Robeson Indians, led by James Chavis and Joseph Brooks, tried in 1934 to obtain congressional legislation naming them the "Siouan Indians of the Lumber River." This legislation had the support both of the Secretary of the Interior and John R. Swanton of the Smithsonian Institution; however, Swanton preferred that the people be given a more specific name than *Siouan* Indians. In a memorandum to Senator Burton K. Wheeler, Chairman of the Senate Committee on Indian Affairs, Swanton wrote:

> The evidence available thus seems to indicate that the Indians of Robeson County who have been called Croatan and Cherokee are descendants of certain Siouan Tribes, of which the most prominent were the Cheraw and Keyauwee. . . It is not improbable that a few families or small groups of Algonquin connection may have cast their lot with this body of people. . . if the name of any tribe is to be used [for] this body of 6 or 8 thousand people, that of the Cheraw would be most appropriate.

Though the idea of the Lumbees being of Siouan descent intrigued many, it gained the support of only a handful of the Lumbee people, and the opposition of most, because it threatened, by offering an imprecise name, to introduce a new element of confusion into their history. Thus, the bill seeking to rename the people was ultimately abandoned and died, but not before it produced some developments that would have future ramifications.

During the same period of interest in the "Siouan" bill, Joseph Brooks wrote to the Commissioner of Indian Affairs, asking what benefits his people would be entitled to if the bill passed. Assistant Commissioner William Zimmerman responded to this inquiry on June 11, 1935, calling particular attention to Section 19 of the Indian Reorganization Act of 1934. This section states:

> The term Indian as used in this Act shall include all persons of Indian descent who are members of any recognized Indian tribe now under Federal jurisdiction, and all persons who are descendants of such members who were, on June 1, 1934, residing within the present boundaries of any Indian reservation, and shall further include all other persons of one-half or more Indian blood.

Zimmerman went on to say in his letter to Brooks, "In order to share in the benefits of this act, your people must fall within the third class." This meant they must prove their Indianness according to an artificial standard established by the Washington bureaucracy, a task of almost insurmountable difficulty unless one's family contained individuals previously recognized as Indians by the federal government.

Because of the complexity of determining "Indianness" on the basis of blood, 209 members of the Indian community in Robeson cooperated with a physical anthropologist, Carl Selezer, who used anthropometry in an attempt to determine who was Indian, according to the criterion established by the government. Anthropometry is the science and technique of human measurements. Selezer attempted to determine Indianness on the basis of anatomical and physiological features. Selezer's findings were later revealed to Joseph Brooks in a letter from John Collier, Commissioner of Indian Affairs. Collier wrote:

> This answers your inquiry as to the result of Dr. Selezer's physical examination of members of the Siouan tribe. A total of 209 individuals were examined, of this total 22 were found, on the basis of the physical test exclusively, to be apparently of one-half or more Indian blood. As you know no other evidence was attainable; no geneaological evidence; no historical documentary evidence; and no etymotological evidence. It is

not in my power to say whether the findings of the physical anthropologist, Dr. Selezer, will by itself be considered by the Secretary of the Interior to supply the necessary evidence for a final decision upon the question at issue, namely as to whether the 22 number of individuals can be declared Indians under the meaning of the Indian Reorganization Act.

On December 12, 1938, another letter was sent to Brooks by Assistant Commissioner Zimmerman, in which he said:

As you may recall, we accepted a total of 209 applications in Robeson County, and of these, 22 applications were recommended for submission to the Secretary. He has ruled that, on the basis of the information presented, the 22 individuals should be considered eligible for enrollment as persons one-half or more Indian, and entitled to benefits established by the Indian Reorganization Act. *Please note* that no other benefits are involved. These people did not obtain tribal status or any rights or privileges in any tribe.

Although the events of the 1930's led the national government to recognize "22" of the examined people as Indians, this was done on the absurd basis of physical appearance, of whether a given individual "looked like" an Indian. This determination was made on the absurd basis that Indians are uniformly alike. In fact, Indians are characterized by variety and diversity, as to language, customs, and mode of living, as well as by physical appearance. Can you describe a Greek, Jew, or a Russian, by his appearance? Only in the most superficial way can this be done, and then the exceptions will almost always equal, if not exceed, the rule. Looking back, it seems incredible that the federal government helped perpetuate the myth and the stereotype that all Indians look alike, but that's exactly what was done. Perhaps the significance of this episode is that it indicates, at least in part, why the government has so frequently bungled Indian affairs.

While the Indians of Robeson County were never designated as the "Siouan Indians of the Lumber River," the conclusion of historical research on this point is that some of the decimated Siouan tribes, losing their health to the white man's diseases and their land to the white man's greed, took refuge in the friendly confines of Robeson's swamps and ultimately were assimilated by the Lumbees with their English culture. This is a reasonable assumption, when one considers that historically the Eastern Sioux were friendly toward all European settlers. However, Siouan influence seems to have consisted of the addition of small numbers of people after they had already abandoned their tribal relationships and begun to adopt the white man's lifestyle.

THE LUMBEE INDIANS AND THE TUSCARORA

In recent years a small segment of the Lumbee population has begun to insist that their heritage is Tuscarora, and to demand that they be recognized by that tribal name. Although the percentage of Indian people who take this stand is small (less than five percent), they have shown themselves to be determined, and at times even violent. Their position is essentially this: That if they are recognized as Tuscarora Indians, they would be entitled to all the forms of assistance provided to "recognized" tribes by the Bureau of Indian Affairs, assistance not provided the Lumbees because of their past self-sufficiency and the fact that they were not a federally-recognized tribe until 1956, when the Congress denied them privileges granted most other Indian people. On the other hand, the historic Tuscaroras, most of whose descendants now live on a reservation in upstate New York, have long been recognized by the national government, and receive federal aid. The discontented Lumbee group seeks to be considered as the North Carolina branch of that tribe, and thus to become eligible for similar benefits.

Yet, it would be misleading to imply that the Tuscarora faction is interested only in federal monies, for this is not the case. There is also a desire, stated by some of their leaders at various times, to end forever the speculation concerning their Indian origins. Their claim to Tuscarora descent rests on two major grounds. First, they believe that Tuscaroras moved into the Robeson area during the period of the Tuscarora War, either to escape enslavement or to avoid further hostilities, and in the process became a factor in the existing society. Second, they rely on the fact that in

21

the 1930's, the Department of the Interior conducted physical examinations in the area in an effort to gauge the Indianness of the people and concluded that 22 of the test group of 209 were Indian by artificial government standards. Since several of the discontented faction are descended from those individuals, they claim the Tuscarora name to substantiate their position that they are Indian. Unfortunately, they have adopted the attitude that they are the only legitimate Indians in the area and insist that any funds appropriated for the Indians of the county should be used for their benefit alone.

The position taken by the Tuscarora faction is almost impossible to reconcile with the facts. It is most unlikely that there were more than a few, if any, Tuscarora Indians in the Robeson area prior to the war of 1711-1713. The records show that the first European settlers, arriving in 1731, found a people fully assimilated to the white man's lifestyle. It is therefore difficult to see how the Robeson "Tuscaroras" can claim to be the only Indians in the area, since the group from which they claim descent must have been late comers and few in number, making little impact on the society of which they became a part. But the biggest puzzle is how the Tuscarora faction can utilize the developments of the 1930's which were supposed to show kinship with the Eastern Sioux, and use these developments to "prove" their own descent from the historic Tuscarora. This is particularly confusing for two reasons: First, the Eastern Sioux and the historic Tuscaroras were hereditary enemies, a fact that virtually rules out any substantial Tuscarora activity or influence in Robeson, since its location is within what were Siouan lands; second, physical examinations to prove racial characteristics are, at best, of questionable value but most certainly cannot prove tribal origin. There is some evidence, however, based on oral tradition and fragmented documents, that Tuscarora blood was marginally infused into the local Indian society in the decades following the defeat of that nation in 1713.[3] In summary, Tuscarora influence was piecemeal, minor and contributory, rather than major and formative in the history of the Indian people of Robeson County.

---

3. The evidence indicates that marriage was the principal method by which the Tuscarora strain was introduced into the Lumbee community in the eighteenth century.

CONCLUSIONS

The central fact of Lumbee history is that the people are Indian in origin and social status. That the Lumbees believe in their Indianness has done a great deal to shape their history and way of viewing the world in which they live. Moreover, the Lumbees, more than most native Americans, are well aware that being Indian is not merely a physical foundation, but that it is even more importantly a state of mind, a self-concept. Consequently, the Lumbees, now more than ever, are determined to achieve political, social, and economic equality with the whites, while at the same time preserving their distinctiveness as a people.

Although it is true that the Lumbees have no visible "Indian culture," such as dances or a native language, outward manifestations are not the only way to determine ethnic identity. There are traits which are characteristic of American Indians which are still found in the Lumbee community despite the tremendous cultural impact of whites in the past. No one who really knows the Lumbee people can possibly deny their firm attachment to the land, nor fail to note their inherent religiousness, nor dismiss the sense of unity that exists when outsiders pose a threat. While it is true that Lumbees accept the idea of private property, as do many other modern Indians, they nevertheless part with their land only with great reluctance and usually out of extreme need. While it is true that they follow the teachings of Christianity, their religion is not just a philosophy to be practiced on Sunday, but rather an all-encompassing way of life. Finally, while it's true that many ethnic minorities are protective-minded, Indians, including the present-day Lumbees, are notoriously individualistic until some external danger overrides this characteristic and causes them to function as a unit, a phenomenon anthropologists refer to as "the massing effect." Thus, the Lumbees are Indian because of their history, their self-image, their status in society, and in many of their characteristics.

In conclusion, it seems incontestable that the Lumbee Indians are the product of an environment that produced a swamp-surrounded island of land, which in turn afforded isolation and protection and brought together in one community remnants both of the "Lost Colony" and several Indian tribes, of which the Hatteras and various Eastern Siouan peoples were the most prominent. While there are some who will find the conclusion of amalgamation unsatisfactory, it is the only conclusion possible in light of the facts, traditions of the people, and logic of the situation. The origins of the Lumbee Indians should no longer be viewed as lost.

The Lumbee River. Still known as Drowning Creek on its upper reaches, it has taken its toll of lives with its swift-running, black waters. It was at this site that James Lowrie began to operate a ferry in 1791.

—Photo by William P. Revels

"FREE AND INDEPENDENT SOVEREIGNS"

Our ancestors found these people, far removed from the commotions of Europe, exercising all the rights and enjoying the privileges of free and independent sovereigns of this new world. . . The white men, the authors of all their wrongs, approached them as friends. . . and, being then a feeble colony and at the mercy of the native tenants of the soil, by presents and profession propitiated their good will. The Indian yielded a slow but substantial confidence; granted to the colonists an abiding place; and suffered them to grow. . . And now he finds that this neighbor, whom his kindness nourished. . . turns upon him and says, "Away! we cannot endure you so near us! These forests and rivers, these groves of your fathers, these firesides and hunting grounds are ours by the right of power and the force of numbers.". . . I ask who is the injured and who is the aggressor?. . Do the obligations of justice change with the color of the skin?

—THEODORE FRELINGHUYSEN[1] (1830)

1. Frelinghuysen was a United States senator from New Jersey who opposed the removal of the eastern Indians on moral, legal and Christian grounds.

2

From Liberty to Repression

Throughout the seventeenth century the Lumbee Indians enjoyed a solitude borne of isolation. The abundance of fish and game, the fertility of their bottom lands, the availability of forest products, and the convenience of the river gave them self-sufficiency. At the same time, nature herself gave them a sense of physical and psychological well-being. The many swamps afforded protection against enemies who might penetrate that natural barrier and refuge. The tall pines, imposing in their height and number, watched over them like silent sentinels, adding to the aura of security that prevailed. Their remoteness from other Indian tribes and from the earliest English settlements was assurance that they would be reasonably untroubled in the 1600's.

But with the coming of the eighteenth century, the seclusion the Lumbees had known for untold years began to end. Momentous developments had already occurred to the north and south. As early as 1650, settlers were steadily drifting down from Virginia into the Albemarle Sound region of North Carolina. Twenty years later, Englishmen, under a charter granted to eight powerful nobles known as the Lords Proprietors, established a colony at Charles Town in South Carolina. The Cape Fear Valley, which included the lands of the Lumbees, lay midway between those two

English settlements. Over the next two generations, pressure for land, a desire for adventure, and the expectation of riches led whites south from Albemarle and north from Charles Town. As new lands were opened, it was only a matter of time before the Lumbee Indians gained neighbors and had to face problems of accommodation.

The tranquility of the Lumbees was initially threatened by Huguenot settlers from lower South Carolina. These French Protestants occupied lands along the Pee Dee River in the early eighteenth century, but apparently had little contact and no lasting influence on the Lumbees. Then, in 1711, according to local tradition, the outbreak of the Tuscarora War brought a few whites with their Indian allies marching through Robeson County along a Lumbee trail later known as the "Lowrie Road." As noted in Chapter One, controversy surrounds the question of whether the Tuscarora War had a direct impact on the Lumbee people or not. Unquestionably, the defeat of the Tuscaroras had an indirect effect, since vast new lands were opened for white settlement, and these lands bordered the Cape Fear Valley. The next step for colonists was obviously into the virgin territory of southeastern North Carolina, and that step was taken by the Highland Scots. Their appearance shattered the peace of the Lumbees and carried them irrevocably into the mainstream of colonial life.

At the arrival of the first whites, the Lumbee Indians had an essentially European culture. As already stated, they spoke English lived in English-style housing, and farmed in the English manner. Yet, there was one custom they practiced that was decidedly Indian—the Lumbees possessed their lands in common, having no concern for metes and bounds and fee simple titles. It was only with the coming of the Scots that they began to lay out boundaries and seek deeds to the property. Undoubtedly this became necessary if they were to retain the lands they had cleared and long cultivated.

Although the evidence to be gained from early land grants and titles is limited, it is sufficient to show that Lumbee ancestors were acquiring such documents as early as the 1730's.[1] James Lowrie

1. Tradition has it that there are older deeds than those of the 1730's but the authors have been unable to locate any.

and Henry Berry received land grants directly from King George II of England in 1732, the former receiving a second grant in 1738.[2] In fact, James Lowrie ultimately possessed an estate of over two thousand acres and was for many years one of the more substantial landowners in the area. Two Lumbee ancestors who bought land in the 1730's were John Brooks, who took title to one thousand acres in 1735, and Robert Lowrie, who purchased six hundred and forty acres in 1736. In the remaining decades of the century, land deeds proliferated, showing clearly that the Lumbees were accepting the concept of private property and some were acquiring considerable holdings. The lands to which the Indians took title were usually located by their relationship to the Lumbee River or to a prominent swamp, such as Ashpole Swamp, Long Swamp, or Back Swamp, all of which are unmistakably in Robeson County. Moreover, the surnames on the titles remain prominent among the Lumbees to this day, such as Locklear, Oxendine, Bell, Cumbo, Hunt, and Chavis, as well as those previously mentioned. When the first federal census was taken in 1790, there were at least eighty-five families of Lumbees in the classification "all free persons not white." Given the fragmented nature of early public records, neither the land deeds nor census records provide a complete accounting of the Lumbees in southeastern North Carolina, but they do unequivocally establish their presence and their roles as tillers of the soil.

While white relations with the Indians of North America generally constituted a sorry record of false promises, misuse, and the playing off of Indians against Indians, or, in some instances, the pitting of Indians against blacks to prevent any kind of minority alliance, Lumbee-white relations were generally serene. Indeed, with acceptance of the concept of private property, the most visible difference between the Lumbees and their new neighbors

---

2. It is noteworthy that throughout Lumbee history there have been variant spellings of several surnames that are prominent in the Indian community—Lowrie, Lowry, Lowery; Locklear, Lockileer, Locklaer, Chavis, Chevers, Chavers; Dial, Dyal; and so forth. The variations are sometimes confusing but of no particular significance. For example, all Lowries, regardless of the spelling, are believed descended from this original grantee. It is also a curious fact that one of the "lost colonists" was named Henry Berry. Based on the evidence now available, historians can only speculate on the significance of similarities such as this, but they are intriguing.

was in skin color, not in status or occupation. Interestingly, during the colonial period, since there were no decided cultural differences to set them apart, the Lumbees apparently experienced little discrimination because of their darker hue. Since the colonial definition of an Indian was cultural rather than racial (that is, an Indian was a person with an Indian way of life), the Lumbees' difficulties with the newcomers were essentially economic in nature. In short, the Lumbees found themselves having to protect the lands they claimed from competitors, but as equals, not as "inferior savages." By contrast, the native Americans who lacked the rudiments of a European culture found themselves viewed as obstacles by the colonists, as objects of scorn and disdain, a people "little better than Beasts in Human Shape" who must be shoved aside in the name of progress. Few settlers were as honest as John Lawson, who correctly assessed the situation when he wrote, "We have abandoned our Native Soil, to drive them out, and possess theirs." The Lumbee Indians were more fortunate. So long as cultural factors were the basis of Lumbee-white relationships, the differences that existed were manageable, but, as will be shown later, during the early nineteenth century Southern whites began to base acceptability and equality on color. As this trend became more pronounced, the Lumbees began to suffer from the poison of prejudice.

The kinds of problems the Lumbees faced in the eighteenth century are illustrated by several developments. In 1754, North Carolina made preparations to send troops to help Virginia in her war against the Indians of the back country. Arthur Dobbs, North Carolina's royal governor, asked his agent in each county in the province to report on the availability of men for military service and on the status of the Indians. As found in *The Colonial Records of North Carolina*, the governor's agent in Bladen County, which included Robeson County at the time, responded to the request for information with the following statement:

> Drowning Creek [Lumbee River] on the head of Little Pee Dee, fifty families, a mixt crew, a lawless people, possessing the land without patent or paying any quit rents; shot a surveyor for coming to view vacant lands, Quakers [as to] muster or paying. . .

The report shows that the Lumbees felt a desperate need to protect their lands. They understood the peril of losing their lands; and in an act of self-preservation, they shot a surveyor. The reference to a "mixt crew" indicates the manner in which the Lumbee people were viewed. As previously explained, the Lumbees' lack of an Indian culture meant simply that under the colonial definition they weren't assigned to that category. The government agent who wrote the report was not denying the Indian blood of the people. He was indicating that culturally they had been assimilated, thus offering additional evidence in support of the theory of amalgamation. Bluntly, the governor wanted information on tribal Indians, and the agent who prepared the report obviously found none. Further affirmation of the Lumbees' equality with the whites is the fact that they were eligible for military service, but in this period, like the Quakers, they preferred to be left alone. In fact, prior to the American Revolution, the Lumbees seem to have been uninvolved in the numerous wars of the eighteenth century, whether they originated with the whites or the Indians.

Other than forcing the Lumbees to take action to preserve their lands and resist conscription into the military, the coming of the whites had another indirect effect on the Indians of Robeson County. Like all Indians, the Lumbees were self-reliant, before the European influx. They depended on their ingenuity and the resources of nature for economic survival. Afterwards, they became increasingly dependent on the whites for products they adopted but could not themselves manufacture. Guns, powder, and shot are the most obvious examples of the new dependency, but it extended to many implements, especially those involving metalwork. Once the Indians, including the Lumbees, became reliant on the Europeans for essentials, their lifestyles were permanently altered. Since the Lumbees were already largely acculturated, this development affected them less profoundly than other Indians, but it did affect their economy and their social relations.

Unfortunately, for most Native Americans, the Europeans brought rum to the New World, which quickly became a social problem. They also brought epidemic diseases, which devastated tribal Indians who had no hereditary resistance to the virulent strains that periodically spread among them. The ravages of both were calamitous. Again however, the Lumbees found themselves more fortunate than their Indian brothers. Apparently their white ancestry gave them some awareness of the dangers of liquor and some natural immunity to smallpox and other deadly diseases. By contrast and as a representative example, the Catawbas, once the most powerful of the Eastern Sioux peoples and a nation whose territory theoretically included the Lumbee River region, were reduced to impotence and obscurity by the combination of liquor and germs. In 1738 and again in 1759, smallpox epidemics decimated the population of the southeastern Indians, especially the Catawba who had regular trade with the settlers. Concerning the epidemic of 1759, the *South Carolina Gazette* reported,

> It is pretty certain that the smallpox has lately raged with great violence among the Catawba Indians, and that it has carried off near one-half of that nation, by throwing themselves into the river as soon as they found themselves ill. This distemper has since appeared among the inhabitants of the Cheraws and Waterees, where many families are down, so that unless especial care is taken, it must spread through the whole country, the consequences of which are much to be dreaded. . .

Among the consequences of these epidemics was the disappearance of some traditional tribes and the consolidation of others. During this period it is probable that a few of the more assimilated tribal Indians, such as a small number of the Cheraws or Catawbas, fled into the swamps of Robeson County and merged with the Lumbee community.

Liquor also took its toll, wreaking havoc in many Indian societies. At a meeting with white officials on May 26, 1756, in Salisbury, North Carolina, the great Catawba leader King Haiglar said on this issue,

> I desire a stop may be put to the selling strong Liquors by the White people to my people especially near the Indian Nation. If the White people make strong drink let them sell it to one another or drink it in their own Families. This will avoid a great deal of mischief which otherwise will happen from my people getting drunk and quarreling with the White people. Should any of my people do any mischief to the White people

> I have no strong prisons like you to confine them for it. Our
> only way is to put them under the ground and all these men
> (pointing to his Warriors) will be ready to do that to those
> who shall deserve it.

But liquor was a profitable item in the Indian trade, and its abundance increased rather than diminished; so did its disastrous effects. During the last third of the eighteenth century, only the Lumbee Indians remained a notable force in eastern North Carolina and in the west only the Cherokees continued to be a powerful tribal people. However, the Lumbees were now surrounded by whites, with nowhere to retreat should the need arise.

THE CLASH OF ARMS

When the American colonists declared their independence from England in July, 1776, they knew that a full-scale war was likely to follow, that the British would not passively accept such an imperial loss. Since many colonists chose to remain loyal to the mother country or adopted a position of neutrality, the Rebels were willing to take help wherever it could be found. Although they did not play a pivotal role in the outcome of the conflict, a number of Lumbee Indians, acting as individuals, did take part in the American Revolution on the side of independence, thus contributing to the formation of this nation. As described in his claim for a Revolutionary War pension, John Brooks "served at various times on tours of from three to six months each as a private under Captains Alexander McNeill, Gibson and Hadley and Colonel Regan in the North Carolina Troops." He was "in an engagement at 'Betties Bridge' and in the battle of Camden, where he and Captain Gibson, under whom he was then serving, were captured, taken to Saint Augustine and held for about four months." Brooks was discharged at the close of the war, all of his service having been "rendered in the Cape Fear country." This Indian soldier from Robeson County was awarded a pension and one hundred and sixty acres of land for his part in the struggle against the English.

Two other Lumbees who took an active part in the Revolution were Jacob Locklear and Samuel Bell.[3] Serving as a common soldier, Locklear was a participant in the Battle of Eutaw Springs in upper South Carolina. This battle resulted from General Nathaniel Green's efforts to clear the Carolinas of British troops in 1781. Although the British won the engagement, they did so at considerable cost of manpower, thereby further demoralizing forces that had seen the Americans steadily improving as soldiers and enlarging the territories they controlled. Samuel Bell fought in several skirmishes with Loyalists in the Cape Fear country, the most notable of which was the so-called Battle of Raft Swamp in Robeson County. In the Spring of 1781 Lord Cornwallis, having given up his attempt to take North Carolina, marched his army of regulars into Virginia. But the Loyalists, led by the notorious Colonel David Fanning, continued the struggle. To their chagrin, they suffered a thorough defeat in late summer at Elizabethtown, a small community on the Cape Fear River. In retaliation, Fanning, aided by Colonel Hector McNeil, staged a raid into Robeson County. They surprised a small band of Rebels moving horses through Raft Swamp, and attacked. The fighting was fierce, both men and horses becoming casualties. When the battle was over, Fanning's forces were victorious and the rout at Elizabethtown had been avenged. Yet, in the end, this show of Loyalist strength only caused the Rebels to launch a concerted and successful effort to break Loyalist power in southeastern North Carolina. Forces under General Griffith Rutherford swept the Loyalists from the Cape Fear country in the autumn of 1781. With the surrender of Cornwallis to General Washington in Virginia during this same time, the war ended.

North Carolina was an important battlefield during the Revolutionary War, and her citizens, regardless of race, suffered from the problems of devastation, political factionalism, and economic disruption. In many ways, however, the most difficult problem to overcome was that of animosity between the citizens who fought for freedom and those who favored retaining union with Britain.

---

3. In addition to John Brooks, Jacob Locklear, and Samuel Bell, the pension records show that James Brooks, Berry Hunt, Thomas Jacobs, Michael Revels, Richard Bell, Primus Jacobs, Thomas Cummings and John Hammond served in the Revolutionary War. Where and in what capacity they served is not known. Moreover, oral tradition indicates that there were yet other Lumbees who participated but specifics are totally lacking.

As a result of the split between the Rebels and Loyalists, friends became enemies and families were broken up, sometimes pitting father against son and brother against brother. These kinds of wounds proved the most difficult to heal. The Lumbees, having fought with the victorious Rebels, suffered no ill effects from this internecine division. In fact, A. W. McLean, in his "Historical Sketch of the Indians of Robeson County," argues that the Lumbees benefited from the Revolution and more precisely from the split among the white citizenry. McLean wrote concerning the Lumbees and the War:

> During the Revolution some of these Indians served in the Continental ranks, as well as in the more local organizations raised by the State of North Carolina.
>
> The territory embraced in Robeson County was much divided in sentiment, and toward the close of the Revolution it was the scene of a murderous civil warfare of unparalleled atrocity.
>
> The tradition of these people (the Lumbees) that some of their leaders fought on the side of the Colonies seems to be corroborated by certain circumstances. Giles Leitch says that during the Revolution some of these families acquired a considerable number of slaves. Had they acquired them from North Carolinians, these slaves would have been recovered on the return of peace. Such slaves as the British captured, they sent either to Florida or Nova Scotia. It is therefore probable that these slaves held by these Robeson County Indians were acquired from South Carolina. (Francis) Marion raised his celebrated band largely in that part of North Carolina, and as an inducement for serving with him he offered as pay to his North Carolina troopers slaves taken from the South Carolina Loyalists. So many of these slaves were thus taken and held by his North Carolina troopers that after the war the question of their return became a matter of State Legislation.
>
> After the war, feeling against the local Tories ran so high that they were discriminated against and severe tests of loyalty were applied. There seems to have been no feeling against these Indians, for although not white they were allowed to vote as "freemen," without any change being made in the law to include them. . . Had they been of the Tory element prob-

ably they would not have been allowed the right of suffrage, because the feeling against the Tories was very bitter, especially in that region where they lived.

Much of McLean's information was derived from conversations and interviews with aged Indians. Whether he realized it or not is uncertain, but this future governor of the state added a new possibility to the role of the Lumbees in the Revolution. By implication, he suggests that some served with Francis Marion, the famous guerilla leader of South Carolina. Considering that Marion, "the Swamp Fox," often took refuge on a plantation at Red Banks amidst the Lumbees, this is certainly a strong possibility. However, because of a lack of solid evidence, this remains unproven and is perhaps unprovable.

In 1801 the new nation seemed stable, the capable Thomas Jefferson was president, and the future seemed bright for all but America's slave population. But clouds soon appeared on the horizon. Napoleon Bonaparte was the ruler of France, and by 1804 he was no longer able to hold his boundless ambition in check. War broke out on the continent and in the next four years "the Little Corporal" made himself the master of Europe. Only the British, through their control of the seas, were able to resist military conquest or domination by the Emperor of France. Although the United States tried to stay out of the Napoleonic Wars by following a policy of neutrality, both England and France violated America's neutral rights in their efforts to destroy each other, especially after they adopted strategies of economic warfare. Because the British violations were more flagrant, especially the impressment of sailors from American ships, and because many Americans had come to desire Canada, the United States finally, in 1812, abandoned neutrality and declared war on England. North Carolina played a very limited role in that war, being chiefly concerned about the danger of British attacks along the coast and the possible renewal of frontier warfare with the Cherokees, a fear that never materialized. Having been accepted as citizens and equals for some years, the Lumbees rallied to the support of the state when the call went out for volunteers. The volume *Muster Rolls of the Soldiers of the War of 1812; Detached from the Militia of North Carolina* shows that at least eight Lumbees were in the army during that conflict.[4] However, like most other North Carolinians in the military, these Indian soldiers saw no action. Their primary role was to be prepared should the British invade Wilmington or some other coastal location. Actually, a total of eighteen North Carolinians were killed in combat in the war, as contrasted with the hundreds of casualties elsewhere.

THE TRIUMPH OF INJUSTICE

According to traditional interpretation, the War of 1812 is important for freeing the United States culturally and economically from England and because the national honor was defended against British depredations, though Canada was not won, as some had hoped. From the American Indian's standpoint, the war period marked the beginning of years of tragedy. For some time the Shawnee leader Tecumseh had been trying to organize a defensive tribal confederacy to resist the westward sweep of white settlement. His successes in the midwest alarmed frontier settlers and they began to call upon General William Henry Harrison, governor of the Territory of Indiana, to raise an army and destroy the Indian capital on Tippecanoe Creek. While Tecumseh was in the southeast, trying unsuccessfully to convince his mother's people, the Creeks, to join him, his brother, The Prophet attacked Harrison's army, was beaten back in a fierce day-long battle, and the village at Tippecanoe was razed. Many settlers accused the English of supplying Tecumseh's followers with arms and food. Anti-British and anti-Indian sentiment became intertwined, prior to 1812, to the detriment of the Indians.

When the Anglo-American war began, Tecumseh sided with the British, believing they would demand less from the Indians than their opponents. In 1813, Tecumseh was killed at the Battle of the Thames, depriving the Indians of an exceptional leader and destroying the remnants of his confederation. Ironically, even be-

---

4. Although there may have been others, the muster rolls contain the names of Charles Oxendine, Thomas Locklier, John Drinkwater, Hugh Locklier, William Bullard, Elias Bullard, Richard Bullard, and Stephen Cumbo.

fore his death, his prediction of the future was becoming reality. In the summer of 1813, a Creek war faction known as the "Red Sticks," whose support Tecumseh had tried to enlist to no avail, rose up along the southern frontier in an effort to stop encroachment on their lands. The fighting in Alabama led to the Creek War of 1813-1814 and brought Andrew Jackson with a combined force of Tennessee militia and Cherokee Indians into the area. In the Battle of Horseshoe Bend, Jackson broke the Creeks' power and they capitulated. Under the Treaty of Fort Jackson (August 9, 1814) signed by only a portion of the Creeks, two-thirds of the Creek lands were ceded to the United States, and the Indians were forced to withdraw from the western and southern parts of Alabama. Several weeks earlier, the Indians of the Old Northwest had signed the Treaty of Greenville, restoring peace with the American government and compelling five tribes to go to war against the British. These battles and treaties were an indication of a new attitude developing among the whites toward the eastern Indians. Quite simply, as the whites looked westward they found the Indians in their way and they began to argue that the logical solution was for the Indians to move. From being the original inhabitants, the Indians had become strangers in their own land. The roots of the later policy of removal can be detected in these events and with the personalities, notably that of Jackson, who were involved. Although the Lumbees were far removed from the frontier and its problems, the feelings of hostility toward Indians that were becoming visible could only be harmful to all Indians, regardless of their location or previous condition.

In 1819, the United States was shaken by controversy when the territory of Missouri applied for admission to the Union as a slave state. The idea of allowing slavery to expand into new lands was reprehensible to many Americans, but to allow the precarious balance that existed in the Senate to be broken in favor of the South was unthinkable. Though the dispute was finally resolved through compromise, it made sectionalism a definite part of American politics and pushed slavery to the front as the most emotional issue the nation had ever known. In the future, southerners would become ever more preoccupied with slavery, and as a logical outcome, they became dangerously color conscious.

A desire to extinguish Indian titles in the east and a hardening of racial attitudes toward blacks in the South both came to a head in the 1830's during the administrations of Andrew Jackson. In 1830 the Congress of the United States passed the Indian Removal Act and President Jackson signed it.[5] The provisions of this act applied to all tribal Indians east of the Mississippi River and basically required that they abandon their tribal existence or remove to the west. Through intimidation, bribery, and force, except for a few bands of Seminoles able to hold out in the vastness of the Everglades, the traditional eastern tribes were compelled to leave their homes. The Cherokee "Trail of Tears" was known to a greater or lesser extent by all their brothers. By 1835, despite military and legal resistance, the final doom of eastern Indians could no longer be averted.

In the early 1830's, the question of slavery also reappeared in national politics, partly as an aspect of what would be a continuing dispute over states' rights, but mainly as an independent issue. On January 1, 1831, William Lloyd Garrison issued the first edition of his abolitionist newspaper *The Liberator*. The slavery question would not again slip into the dark recesses of the national mind. Then, eight months later, the visionary Nat Turner staged his insurrection in Southampton County, Virginia. For ten days all southern eyes and thoughts were focused on Virginia and what this development portended. When it became known that fifty-seven whites were dead, the South recoiled in mournful shock. Always frightened at the prospect of slave uprisings, the whites of the Old South would not again sleep easy. Never mind that few slaves joined Turner's uprising, or that approximately one hundred Negroes were killed in the manhunt that captured him, or that Turner and nineteen others were tried and executed. Garrison and Turner together traumatized the ante-bellum South and henceforth all non-whites would pay for the fears they had fired.

Against the backdrop of Indian removal and anxieties over slave plots, North Carolinians in 1834 voted to call into session a

---

5. In what was a masterpiece of bureaucratic insensitivity, the federal government chose to name U.S. Highway 74, which runs through the traditional lands of both the Lumbee and Cherokee Indians, the Andrew Jackson Highway.

constitutional convention, the purpose of which was to amend the organic law of the state in the direction of democracy. Specifically, the people of the western counties had long decried their lack of an effective voice in the government, and were now demanding representation based on population, as well as the direct popular election of their governor. The eastern counties, which had long dominated the government, wanted to pacify the west, but without giving up their control. The delegates to the North Carolina Constitutional Convention of 1835 did what all good politicians do when there is an impasse—they compromised. On the important question of representation, the Convention agreed that the upper house, or Senate, should be based on wealth and property, which would allow the east to control it; and that the lower chamber, or House of Commons, should be based on population, which gave the west control. Amendments were approved allowing direct election of the governor and the sheriffs, abolishing borough representation, and providing an easier method for changing the constitution. Finally, the delegates turned their attention to the question of "whether any, and if any, what amendments are proper to be made to the said Constitution, as to the abrogation or restriction of the right of free negroes or mulattoes to vote for members of the Senate or House of Commons." The original state constitution of 1776 required that voters be freemen and meet certain property qualifications, but it made no mention of race if otherwise eligible. When the delegates to the 1835 Convention turned their attention to this question, they gave it little serious consideration, their actions being dictated mainly by their fears. Among the most frequently cited reasons for proposing that the free Negroes should be disfranchised were that the Bill of Rights "did not apply to men of colour," that ". . . this is a nation of white people—its offices, honors, dignities and privileges are alone open to, and to be enjoyed by, white people," that the Negro vote is "easily bought," that free Negroes "lack intelligence and moral character," and to allow the Negro the vote in North Carolina would make the state "the asylum of free negroes; they will come in crowds, from the North, South, and West, and we shall be overrun by a miserable and worthless population." In the end, the delegates, in a surprisingly close vote of 66 to 61, agreed to an amendment that read as follows: "No free negro, free mulattoe, or free person of mixed blood, descended from negro ancestors to the fourth generation inclusive (though one ancestor of each generation may have been a white person) shall vote for members of the Senate or House of Commons." When the various amendments were submitted to the people, they ratified them by a total of 26,771 for, to 21,606 against.

The Lumbee Indians watched the developments of the previous twenty years with some uneasiness; and yet they could not bring themselves to be unduly alarmed. After all, they were not tribal Indians subject to removal. They had long enjoyed the prerogatives and met the responsibilities of citizenship, and the new constitution said nothing about depriving Indians of any rights they possessed. But the Lumbees misread the signs; the future was not going to be like the past. The authorities were pouring a cup of misery for all non-whites. Whatever distinctions that had existed in the past would be erased with a singlemindedness of purpose that was awesome in its implications for the Lumbee Indians.

CONCLUSIONS

In the century between the coming of the Scots and the adoption of the Revised Constitution of 1835, the Lumbee Indians saw their protected enclave invaded. They experienced new problems of accommodation which, on the whole, they peacefully resolved. They took part in two great wars against the British, and they witnessed the rise of two variant but related strains of racism —one aimed at the Indians because they had lands the whites wanted, and the other aimed at the Negroes because they were a threat to the southerners' belief in white supremacy and the society they created around that belief. Although the Lumbees generally were innocent onlookers to these dreadful developments, in the years that followed they found themselves caught up in a whirlwind of emotion and prejudice. When calm finally returned to North Carolina four decades later, the dust of discrimination that whipped about so furiously had been settled by an outpouring of blood.

41

HENRY BERRY LOWRIE

THE HERO OF A PEOPLE

Henry Berry Lowrie where are you?
Sleeping in an unknown grave.
Does the grass grow above your breast,
Or do dark waters flow
With secret sounds through your bones
That will confuse mankind
Until the end of time.
From ever lasting to everlasting
You are the hero of a people.
Keep your secrets as you sleep—
That is part of your greatness.

—ADOLPH L. DIAL

3

A Time of Troubles

Having been a self-sufficient and non-reservation people, the Lumbee Indians were accepted as free men in North Carolina prior to 1835. After that date, however, the darkening racial mood of the Old South began to alter their status for the worse. Although the intent of the 1835 Constitution, as noted, was to disfranchise free Negroes and mulattoes, the Indians of Robeson County soon found themselves deprived of their political and civil rights simply because they weren't white, in a society and region that had become intensely color conscious. Thus, the adoption of an amendment that had nothing to do with them originally signaled the beginning of decades of harassment and suppression. Fear of a social system in which all men were free and equal overwhelmed the reason of the South's leaders and instilled in them a determination to control absolutely the non-white segments of their population. Southerners convinced themselves that "white supremacy" was essential to the continuance of their way of life. Consequently, and ironically, what is known nationally as the "Age of Jacksonian Democracy" was in truth an age of suspicion, hostility, and subjugation for the South's minority races: North Carolina was no exception to these attitudes and practices. The ruling element of the state adopted the position that all non-whites were dangerous, and shut their eyes and hearts to the immorality of the course they pursued.

The implication of these events was not lost on the Lumbees. The Indians quickly perceived that the whites intended to treat them as inferiors, a role they steadfastly refused to accept. Feeling betrayed by a people they had frequently helped in the past and never harmed, the Lumbees grew increasingly antagonistic toward the whites in the years after 1835. Indeed, the racial split that began to develop in the 1830's finally culminated in open rebellion in the 1860's.

Harassment of Lumbees in the ante-bellum period was both legal and economic. In 1835 Charles Oxendine, a Lumbee, physically attacked Alfred Lowry, another Lumbee, and was taken to court on charges of assault and battery, trespassing, and disturbing the peace. Oxendine pleaded guilty and was fined fifteen dollars, which he was unable to pay. Invoking an 1831 law, the judge then ruled that since the defendant could not pay his fine, the sheriff of the county should hire him out "to any person who will pay the fine for his services for the shortest space of time." Oxendine, believing that the law which permitted the practice of "hiring out" violated his rights as a free man and was therefore unconstitutional, appealed his case to the North Carolina Supreme Court. In the case of the *State v. Oxendine* (1837) the Supreme Court evaded the question of the validity of the law, on a technical point. It ruled that the penalty of "hiring out" could be imposed only when the defendant had been "convicted" of a violation of the criminal laws of the state. The court further decreed that a "conviction" occurred only when there was a confession or a trial in which the facts of the case were argued. Because Oxendine pleaded guilty, he was not technically convicted. The state's highest court concluded that the Superior Court "erred" in its judgment and instructed it to impose a penalty compatible with common law. Rather than incur further expenses in the matter, the local authorities dropped the case.

Although the state supreme court declined to take a stand concerning the 1831 law, Justice William Gaston, who wrote the majority opinion in the *Oxendine Case* and who was more liberal than most of his fellow Carolinians, did take the opportunity to state that the law in question was "highly harsh in its character" and to note that laws dealing with non-whites smacked of injustice. According to Gaston, whites could commit crimes far more "atrocious" than non-whites and be much less severely punished. Yet, the court as a whole, no doubt influenced by the times, indirectly upheld what was blatantly unfair legislation.

In 1840, the North Carolina General Assembly passed a law which prohibited free non-whites from owning or carrying weapons, without first having obtained a license from the Court of Pleas and Quarter Sessions in their county. The question of bearing arms also eventually made its way to the North Carolina Supreme Court. In 1853, in the case of the *State v. Noel Locklear,* North Carolina's highest court upheld Locklear's conviction for unlawful possession and carrying of firearms and, by implication, affirmed the constitutionality of the discriminatory law under which he was tried.

From an economic standpoint, the Indians were angered because the whites sought ways either to use them as free labor or, worse, to obtain their lands. The Lumbees still refer with bitterness to what are called "tied mule" incidents. Such an incident occurred when a white farmer tied his mule on an Indian's land, freed several cows in the Indian's pasture, and put a hog or two in his pen. Then, the white farmer would arrive with the authorities and claim that the Indian had stolen his animals. Knowing he had little chance for justice in the courts, the Indian would agree to provide free labor for a period of time, so that charges would not be pressed, or to give up a portion of his land as a settlement. This was, of course, only one way in which the Indians were deprived of their labor and property; other, more "sophisticated" quasi-legal means were also used.

THE LOWRIE WAR

Exploitation and injustice naturally intensified the mood of hostility that existed between the races in the ante-bellum period. It was, however, the coming of the Civil War which forced a confrontation between the whites and Lumbees concerning the status of the Indian people. The ambivalence of the Lumbees' position was shown by the fact that some joined the Confederate Army at the outbreak of the war, though whether they were accepted as Indians or passed for white is unknown. Before long, however, the civil authorities began to conscript Lumbees for labor camps at Fort Fisher and other places on the coast. They were used mostly for building batteries and making salt. Many of the Indians in Robeson County refused to serve as forced labor. Ironically, however, they continued for several years to be willing to serve in the Confederate Army, if permitted. Because Fort Fisher was essential to the defense of Wilmington (it was a port suitable for the operation of blockade runners and a primary source of supplies for the Confederate troops in Virginia), every effort was made to complete that defensive complex as soon as possible. Although a few regular troops were used and some civilian white labor, on the whole the Confederacy relied on conscripted Indian labor and slaves. The Lumbees resented the attempts to deprive them of their status and freedom. and found conditions at the labor camps intolerable. Food rations were inadequate, medical facilities almost non-existent; the work was often dangerous and always hard and monotonous. The misery of their circumstances and their pride as freemen led them to flee the coastal work camps for the swamps of Robeson County. There they were joined by others who sought to avoid conscription, and occasionally by Union soldiers who had escaped from a Confederate prison at Florence, South Carolina, a distance of sixty miles from the Lumbee River Indian lands.

Sharing their swamp refuge with the northern escapees brought the Indians into contact with the reality of the war. Whereas earlier they had favored the Confederacy, by the end of 1863 they had come to view that government as oppressive. Consequently, their willingness to help the Union soldiers avoid recapture grew. This, combined with a need for food, led to violent confrontation between several Lumbees and a white Robesonian.[1]

In 1864, a wealthy planter and minor Confederate official,

1. It is important to note that the sources dealing with the Lumbees during the Civil War and Reconstruction periods don't always agree as to sequence, characters, or details. The major sources are newspaper stories, testimony given during investigations, diaries, polemics, and accounts passed down orally. The authors have attempted to corroborate facts where possible.

James P. Barnes, accused several of Allen Lowrie's sons of having stolen and butchered two of his "best hogs," supposedly to feed escaped Union prisoners. Allen Lowrie was a respected and hard-working Lumbee farmer who could trace his ancestry back to the earlier-mentioned James Lowrie who settled in Robeson in the 18th century. While he and his family did, on at least one occasion, befriend Union escapees, no one knows for certain whether his sons stole Barnes' hogs or whether Barnes accused them of it for ulterior motives. At any rate, Barnes claimed he followed cart tracks from his place to the Lowrie's and then discovered two hog ears bearing his identifying mark. He ordered the Lowries to stay off his land or be shot. Apparently Barnes' attempts to intimidate the Lowries, plus his efforts to conscript Indian labor for the Confederacy, led to his death. On December 21, 1864, while going to the Clay Valley Post Office where he was postmaster, Barnes was shot. He fell with a load of buckshot in his side and breast. As his assailants approached, Barnes cried out, "Don't shoot me again— I am a dying man." A young Indian carrying a shotgun replied, "You are the man who swore to kill me" and fired a second load into Barnes' face, tearing away part of his cheek. The dying man's screams brought several neighbors and slaves to his side. He lived just long enough to accuse William and Henry Berry Lowrie, two of Allen's sons, as his attackers.[2] This whole sordid incident reflected the growing racial tension in Robeson County and the increasing rage of the Lumbee people. Barnes' death was simply the first of many violent incidents to follow.

THE CONFLICT GROWS

The Indian's attempts to avoid service at the coast, their growing friendliness with escapees from Florence, and the murder of Barnes, brought them into conflict with the Home Guard. This was an organization of local citizens charged broadly with aiding the Confederate cause and more specifically with maintaining law

---

2. Dr. Earl Lowry, who is writing a history of the Lowry family, blames Barnes' death on whites, but many other Lumbees believe that the two Lowrie youths were responsible for this killing.

and order while so many Southern white men were at war. Unfortunately, many members of the Home Guard saw in the war an opportunity to help themselves, frequently at the expense of the Indians. One of the more notorious members of the Guard was James Brantly Harris, a 230-pound, swaggering, cursing, redfaced bully. Prior to the war, Harris, a white man, trafficked in liquor among the Indians. With the outbreak of war he became an officer in the Home Guard and was charged with keeping the peace in "Scuffletown,"[3] hunting deserters, conscripts and escaped Union prisoners. Harris had an eye for the women and is reputed to have fathered a number of illegitimate children. He is remembered in the folk stories of the Lumbees as a man "mean as the devil, the meanest man in Robeson County." Apparently Harris' first violent dispute with the Lumbees came about because of his attentions to an Indian girl, bitterly resented by her boy friend. The young Indian threatened to kill Brant Harris if he did not leave his girl alone. Harris learned of the threat, and either from apprehension or fury, determined to kill the Indian who had made it. From a night ambush, Brant Harris shot and killed a youth he supposed was his enemy, but he killed the wrong person. He had murdered Jarman Lowrie, the son of George Lowrie and a nephew of Allen Lowrie, brother of the boy he intended to kill. Having moved among the Indians for some time, Harris must have known that he had made sworn enemies of the whole Lowrie family with this act, and that his life was in greater peril than before. What he didn't know was that he had sown seeds of anger which would ultimately yield a harvest of blood and hate.

Since the local authorities ignored the murder of Jarman Lowrie, the personal feud between Harris and the Lowries intensified in the weeks that followed. Harris knew that other Lowries would probably seek to take his life, and he became particularly fearful when two of the boy's brothers were given a few days' furlough from their work at Fort Fisher and arrived home for a visit with their parents. Fearing that they might try to kill him, particularly since he had originally conscripted them, thus giving

---

3. Whether Scuffletown was a precise locaation or the name for any place where the Indians gathered for a good time has never been determined. Some scholars believe it was in the general area of modern Pembroke, others locate it elsewhere, such as at Moss Neck, and some, including the authors of this book, believe that it was a floating or moving community.

them double reason to hate him, Harris, backed by his Home Guard unit, arrested the two on charges of desertion. He told their parents he was taking them to Moss Neck depot to put them on the train back to Wilmington. Before reaching the station, Harris dismissed his escort, saying he could safely take care of this business himself, since the two prisoners were handcuffed. Once the guard was gone he killed the Lowrie brothers with a bludgeon. Harris later claimed they attacked him and that he was forced to defend himself.

Many people, white as well as Indian, attended the funeral for the slain brothers. In a dramatic and moving speech, George Lowrie, the father of the two dead boys, spoke words of historic significance. He said:

> We have always been friends of white men. We were a free people long before the white men came to our land. Our tribe lived in Roanoke in Virginia. When the English came to our land, we treated them kindly. One of our men went to England in an English ship and saw the great country. We took the English to live with us. There is the white man's blood in these veins as well as that of the Indian. In order to be great like the English we took the white man's religion and laws. . . In the fights between the Indians and white men we always fought on the side of white men, yet white men treated us as Negroes. Here are our young men killed by a white man and we get no justice, and that in a land where we were always free.

The people left the funeral with sadness and determination; the Lumbee will to resist injustice was hardening.

Although an inquest was held concerning the double murder, and a warrant issued for Brant Harris' arrest, he never stood trial for his crimes. On Sunday, January 15, 1865, Harris was pleasure riding in his buggy, accompanied by an Indian woman. Shortly after letting his companion off, he was killed by a barrage of gunfire. The Home Guardsman's lifeless body was taken from the buggy, thrown in a well, and covered up.[4] The young Henry Berry

---

4. Another account says that Harris was so hated by the Indian people that he was buried in an unmarked grave, lying north and south, "crossways of the world," rather than east and west as the Lumbees traditionally bury their dead.

Lowrie and the band he was drawing around himself were, depending upon one's viewpoint, accused of or given credit for the assassination of Brant Harris.

A NIGHTMARE OF VIOLENCE

Knowing that the Home Guard could not allow this act of violence and defiance to go unchallenged, many Indians began to prepare for the worst. Since some of the men were in the swamps or at the coast, food was not as abundant as in the past; and because Indians were legally prohibited from owning weapons, guns were scarce. Therefore, Lumbees began to seek out supplies and weapons, preparing to defend themselves. Raids were regularly staged against farms and plantations in the area to acquire the needed items. The white citizenry was angered over this outburst of lawlessness, refusing to recognize that their actions and attitudes for a generation past had helped create the conditions that led up to this moment. As the days passed, more and more of the blame for the robberies and raids was laid to Allen Lowrie and his sons, despite the family's outstandingly respectable reputation among the Indian people. Allen Lowrie was viewed as an intelligent community leader, a church-going Christian, and one of the more prosperous of the Indian people. Yet, despite their position, the Home Guard was convinced that the Lowries were largely responsible for the breakdown of law and order in the county and that they should be punished as an example, one which would be made effective by their prominence.

During the first week of March, 1865, as General William T. Sherman's Union forces crossed into North Carolina, and as the Confederacy came ever closer to defeat, the enmity between the whites and Indians of Robeson County finally exploded into a prolonged nightmare of brutality and bloodshed. On March 3, Home Guardsmen, commanded by Captain Hugh McGreggor, began an indiscriminate roundup of members of the Allen Lowrie family, whom they blamed for many of the lawless acts of the time. The guardsmen arrested Allen Lowrie, his wife Mary, three of their sons—Calvin, Sinclair, and William—, several female members of the family and George Dial, an Indian neighbor. The arrest of the Lowries and Dial marked the beginning of a terrible sequence of events that produced utter tragedy.

Calvin Lowrie was at work in a field when the military company appeared at his place on March 3. In testimony given during a later investigation, he said about that fateful day:

> I saw them coming and went to meet them. Part of them was in my house and yard before I got there, searching the house. When I got there they had taken a shotgun out and a gourd of powder and wanted to know who I was. I said I was a Lowrie and they said I was bad stock and wanted to know if I knew anything about the robbing that was going on through the country. I told I heard it was going on but did not know who it was. They wanted to know if I knew anything about the union prisoners and if I was harboring them. I don't recollect whether I told them I had seen them but had not been harboring them. They searched the smoke house and wanted to know if I fattened all that meat. I told them I did. They acknowledged there they reconned (sic) I did. Said they wanted me to go with them. Then started down to Allen Lowrie, and in going on they saw my rifle which I carried down in the field to shoot crows and took that. Allen Lowrie was at work at his own field and took him along and went on to his place and when I got there, William was there. They wanted to know if they had not been harboring the Yankies or union prisoners. They said they hadn't. . . They took a demijohn with some brandy in out of the house, took William Lowrie's 3 trunks, all of his clothes or about so and his rifle; put them in a cart and took William Lowrie's horse and put in it and tied me and William Lowrie together and took my Mother and Father and all the family and carried us all down to Sinclair Lowrie's. Part of the crowd had been there and searched the house. When we got there they then carried us all down to [Robert] McKenzies.

About eighty men, frustrated and angered by the outcome of the war and over raids and robberies in the neighborhood, had gathered at McKenzie's place. The Lowrie women were locked in the smoke house, but the men were kept outside for questioning. The members of the company accused the Lowries of "highway robbery," of aiding escaped Union prisoners and Conferedate deserters, of having knowledge of hidden caches of guns, munitions, and other weapons, and of having avoided service on the government fortifications near Wilmington.

Although the Lowries denied all charges against them, various members of the Guard kept up the questioning. Robert McKenzie asked Allen Lowrie "if he hadn't told him if he didn't bring up his boys so that he could take them off to the batteries they would get into trouble," to which Allen replied, "the boys are free from me and I cannot rule them." McKenzie then asked if Allen Lowrie hadn't threatened his life, which the elder Lowrie denied, asking McKenzie for proof of that charge. And so it went.

As the day dragged on, William and Calvin Lowrie, still bound together, asked for water. Accompanied by three or four men, they were allowed to go to a nearby well. Calvin Lowrie relates what followed.

> After we got our water William Lowrie and myself stepped to a fence nearby. William pulled a small dirk out of his pantaloons and cut the rope and ran. One man popped a cap at him as he turned the corner of the house. They then jumped over the fence and run into the field where they could see him and fired on him. . . They then cried out they had him and went on down there and got him. Some one wanted to know who it was shot; they said Capt. Baker as well as I understood it. Then said call no names. Then carried me on back to where the company was outside of the yard and handcuffed me and my father together. . .

After the wounded William Lowrie was brought up from the field, John H. Coble, a white preacher and a member of the group, urged him to "tell the truth and not to die with a lie in his mouth; to tell him where the Union prisoners were and if he was not in the robbing with them." William Lowrie continued to deny the accusations. Someone in the company then remarked that if the Lowries had reported the Union prisoners, "they would have given us credit for it but as we had been harboring the Union prisoners we must suffer for it." The Indian men were then locked in the smoke house with the women.

With the Indians confined, an extra-legal session of court was held. The four Lowrie men were tried by a jury picked from the ranks of the military company, found guilty of various charges, and ordered shot. Calvin and Sinclair Lowrie were saved from that fate when it was pointed out that no allegedly stolen property had been found on their farms, that such property had been recovered only at the home shared by Allen and William Lowrie.[5] Moreover, it was stressed that William had been positively identified as a participant in one of the robberies in the area and that Allen was guilty of possessing some of the stolen property. Thus, the guardsmen satisfied themselves that justice was being done.

Following the trial, Allen and William Lowrie were placed in a mule cart driven by Emmanuel Fulmore, a Negro, and taken back to their home place. There, a common grave was dug by Fulmore and several of the company. The two Lowries were blindfolded, tied to a stake, and executed. According to Fulmore, "There was two rounds fired at them by about twelve men. And Allen and William Lowrie were badly shot in the face and breast." The bodies were then thrown into the grave and covered over. Robeson County's "reign of terror" was beginning.

Once Allen and William Lowrie had been disposed of, several members of the company returned to McKenzie's place and informed the surviving Lowries that their loved ones were dead and buried. They told Calvin Lowrie to go with them to hunt Union camps, but it began to rain and they postponed the expedition until the following morning, leaving their prisoners locked up. The next day, Saturday, March 4, some members of the Home Guard came and took Calvin Lowrie and George Dial to look for camps and hiding places used by Federal escapees. Dial showed them a small underground cave, but neither man had the information being sought. Consequently, at different times during the day, both men were jabbed and poked with bayonets, and both were threatened with execution. The Home Guard did finally

---

5. It is a long-standing belief in the Lumbee community that the so-called "stolen" goods used to incriminate Allen and William Lowrie were planted on their farm.

stumble across a "sick Yankee" at the home of Mrs. Amanda Nash, who initially resisted their attempts to take him, but finally gave him up to prevent the company's using force. The soldier was placed in a cart and all the prisoners once again were taken back to McKenzie's.

On Sunday, after two days of terrifying, uncertain confinement, two members of the local Guard went into the smoke house and told the Lowries that if they fed or helped any more Union troops or Confederate deserters, or "if there was any more mischief through that neighborhood they would have to suffer for it, made no difference who did it." The Indian prisoners were finally released, except for Calvin Lowrie who, accompanied by an armed guard, was forced to drive the captured Union soldier to Lumberton. After performing that task, Calvin Lowrie was finally allowed to return home to the sad duty of looking after the remains of his father and brother.

On Monday, March 6, Sinclair and Calvin Lowrie led a party to the grave of their slain kinsmen, disinterred the bodies, washed and dressed them, and gave them a proper burial. Today, in a lonely cemetery just a few hundred yards from the murder scene, a single marker stands as a silent reminder of past injustice. The Lumbees view the grave site with pride, saying "the Lowrie men died for the Indian people."

THE TERROR CONTINUES

Yet, the terrorizing tactics used against the Lowries didn't stop with the double murder of Allen and William. In early April, 1865, a party of the Home Guard, consisting of about twenty-five men, went to Sinclair Lowrie's house, arrested him and informed him that they had been told by a recaptured Union escapee that some twenty-five to thirty guns were concealed on his farm. Lowrie declared he knew nothing of any guns on his place. Several men of the company left, while the others searched the house and grounds. A few minutes later the air was filled with the report of a gun. Concerned, Sinclair Lowrie decided to take a walk and see what was happening. About that time he learned that his mother was missing and his concern increased. As he started out of the yard, according to later testimony, he met a man who asked for a pitcher to get water, and when he asked what the water was for, was told it was being carried to a sick person. The narrative continues:

> . . . he followed after the man about two hundred yards, and in the woods off the road he saw his mother—Mary Lowry—trying to walk. When he went up to her she threw her arms around his neck and being in a very low and frightened condition, he sat down with her, and after resting, tried to get her to walk again but she was so frightened that she fainted away. Then he sent to the house for a blanket to carry her home, which he did. That his Mother said that she was tied up to a tree and blindfolded, and a gun shot over her head.

Mary Lowrie was so treated because the guardsmen believed this would force her to tell them where the guns were concealed and because she refused to say where her other sons were—those hidden in the woods to keep out of the rebel fortifications. One of those sons was Henry Berry Lowrie, and his already bitter rage intensified.

In 1867, when the various outrages against the Lowries were investigated, largely due to the efforts of William Birnie, agent for the Freedmen's Bureau, several members of the Home Guard attempted to justify their actions. Robert McKenzie, to whose place the arrested Lowries were carried and tried, said he took part in the Home Guard operation because his home had been robbed and his family endangered. He contended that much of the "plunder" taken at Allen Lowrie's place was identified by his neighbors as stolen, and that such lawlessness had to stop. McKenzie justified the summary execution of the two Lowrie men, who he claimed "were shot for Highway Robbery, and not for Harboring escaped Union prisoners," on the grounds that "there was a large number of men hid in the swamps, deserters from the Confederate Army, who would come to their rescue."

But the most determined defenders of the killing of Allen and

William Lowrie were two ministers, Reverend John H. Coble and Reverend Luther McKinnon. In a lengthy statement to William Birnie, these two "men of God" noted that the Lowries had always claimed to be and were accepted as Indians, and that they "disdained the idea that they are in any way connected with the African race." They continued, however, to say that the Lowries were "famous" as robbers as far back as the American Revolution. After conceding the Lowries' Indianness and villifying their character, the ministers proceeded with their justification of the Home Guard's acts. They wrote:

> During the late uphappy war, some of them (the Lowries) gave way to the temptation, which the disordered and defenceless condition of the country presented, and engaged in robbing their neighbors. They soon became an organized and armed band. . . The country was defenceless. The Confederate government was not able to protect itself, much less protect its citizens. . . . Indeed, Sir, they were utterly regardless of all law, human and divine. It came to such a pass that gentlemen feared to go into their yard at night lest they should be fired on and shot down. . . . The community-at-large felt that these lawless and outrageous depredations were intolerable and could be borne no longer. And therefore the few men who were at home organized as a Home Guard, under the laws of the State. It went out determined to break up and scatter that band of robbers and house-breakers. . . William Lowrie confessed that he belonged to the gang and. . . gave the names of his accomplices. As to the guilt of the parties there could be no doubt. According to the laws of the State they were guilty of a capital crime. . . The political sentiments of the Lowries had nothing whatever to do with it. They were not regarded as having any political principles, but they were regarded as robbers and house-breakers. Neither were they killed because they harbored Union prisoners. Any such statement is an unqualified falsehood. They were killed for house-breaking and robbery and for nothing else. . . How many such cases the kill- of Allen and William Lowrie prevented, we do not know, but we are fully convinced that under the circumstances it was a necessity. And tho' it was an awful remedy, it was applied not in rage or passion, but in sadness as a dire necessity, and with

the firm conviction that tho' the letter of the law be dead, the spirit of it must be maintained and robbers punished.

Although the Coble-McKinnon statement was offered as an explanation of the Home Guard's actions, it raises more questions than it answered. How, for example, could a vigilante force and its use of violence preserve the "spirit" of the law? Why did the Home Guard continue harassing the surviving Lowries in the weeks that followed, particularly over the questions of hidden weapons, escaped prisoners and refugees from the work camps, if the murder of Allen and William Lowrie restored law and order and if robbery was the only issue? Why were none of the Lowries allowed to be present at their "trial," if justice was the objective? Given the confusion and passions of the Civil War and Reconstruction years, it's unlikely that the full truth will ever be known, but certainly the two ministers' characterization of the Lowries as "utterly regardless of all law, human and divine," was particularly applicable to themselves and their cohorts. Injustice, to which the Indians had long been subjected, became a feature of life for all Robesonians in the war-shattered years of the mid-nineteenth century.

Although the authorities, civil and military, failed ultimately to take any effective action against the participants in the summary trial and execution of Allen and William Lowry, a form of justice was forthcoming—justice by the sword.[6] Whether Henry Berry Lowrie, one of Allen's younger sons, witnessed the killing of his father and brother from a secluded place in the woods, as one Lumbee legend says, or whether he learned of it later, the twenty-year-old man swore vengeance against those responsible for their deaths, and vengeance was his.

The one accurate charge made by the whites of the 1860's was that various bands existed in the swamps and raided some of

6. The Lowries' difficulty in gaining justice is illustrated by the fact that some of the participants in the act were among "the most prominent men of the county;" some were even members of the grand jury that refused to return a "true bill" in the case of Allen Lowry when it was presented for consideration. The Judge Advocate's Office for the Second Military District took the position that "the time of the alleged commission of the crimes imputed, the condition of society at that period and the circumstances of the transactions themselves, all conspires to render it enexpedient (sic) for the military authorities to institute any proceedings looking to a determination of the merits of the case; and it is advised that cognizance of the charges be not taken."

the surrounding farms. While it has been suggested that these bands operated to weaken the Confederacy, in truth, the men who composed them, whether Indians, blacks, or escaped Union prisoners, were concerned with survival under harsh conditions. Politics was a remote consideration at best. As the war drew to a close, the Union troops were able to join Sherman, and the bands became predominantly Indian in composition, the most important being one led by Henry Berry Lowrie. Reacting to the violence against the Indians in like fashion, blood for blood, Henry Berry Lowrie and his "gang" became the scourge of Robeson County for a decade.

Henry Berry Lowrie was no ordinary man. As was noted many times by his contemporaries, he had exceptional intelligence, handsome features, incredible endurance, courage and determination, and pride in himself and his people. His conduct around women was said to be exemplary. He never harmed women, treating them with courtesy and kindness. A correspondent for the *New York Herald* described him as "one of those remarkable executive spirits that arises now and then in a raw community without advantage other than those given by nature."

THE LOWRIE BAND

The facts concerning the exploits of Lowrie and his band are exceedingly difficult to reconstruct. The hatreds and confusions of the war and post-war years, combined with the legends that have grown over the years, have obscured or colored much that happened in that period. Today, a century later, most Lumbees view Lowrie as a "Robin Hood" and most whites see him as the "devil incarnate." While the truth is no doubt somewhere between these two extremes, the fact is that Henry Berry Lowrie dominated Robeson County's history for nearly ten years.

For some months after the end of the Civil War, there was little violence in Robeson County as most citizens, regardless of race, sought to restore a sense of order and stability to their lives. During this time Henry Berry Lowrie was courting his sixteen-year old cousin Rhoda Strong, later known as the "Queen of Scuffletown." Rhoda was the most beautiful girl in the Indian community, remembered as having a very pretty face of fair complexion, with large, dark, mournful eyes, and a well-developed figure. However, it was also recalled that she couldn't write, smoked a pipe, and "rubbed" (used) snuff. Still, given her other attributes, men turned to watch wherever she went.

On December 7, 1865, Henry Berry Lowrie took Rhoda Strong as his bride. The marriage ceremony was performed by a white friend, Hector J. McLean, at the old Lowrie homestead. Several score of relatives and a white neighbor attended the wedding and enjoyed the feast prepared for the occasion. But what began as a joyous event soon became a tragic confrontation. Lieutenant A. J. McNair appeared with a company of the Home Guard and told Henry Berry Lowrie to consider himself their prisoner. After several tense moments Lowrie finally agreed to go. Although McNair had no warrant when he arrested Lowrie, one was drawn the next day, charging him with the murder of James P. Barnes. Originally incarcerated in the Lumberton jail, that structure was quickly ruled out as being too insecure because it had been burned by a detachment of Sherman's army. So Lowrie was removed to the Columbus County jail at Whiteville, about thirty miles away. However, he never stood trial for the crime with which he was charged. How he accomplished it is unknown, but Henry Berry Lowrie escaped from the Whiteville jail, becoming the first man ever to do so. Mary Norment, author of *The Lowrie History*, wrote that "he filed his way out of the grated iron window bars, escaped to the woods with handcuffs on, and made his way back to his wife in Scuffletown." The mystery is where he got the file. Many Lumbees believe it was carried to him by his young wife, concealed in a cake.

In the years to come, Henry Berry and Rhoda would spend more time apart than together. Yet, they did have three children —Sally Ann, Henry Delaware, and Nellyann. The days would come when Lowrie would express his longing for a peaceful life with his family. Whether Rhoda remained faithful to Henry Berry during their many forced separations is uncertain, but it is known that many men, drawn by her physical attractions, sought to se-

View of the Henry Berry Lowrie house as it looks today, only slightly altered over the past century. Only a few hundred yards from this place, the Home Guard summarily executed Henry Berry's father, Allen, and his brother, William, after (according to legend), forcing them to dig their own graves. As a result of this episode Henry Berry Lowrie swore vengeance on those responsible and from 1864 to 1874 waged war in Robeson County.

—Photo by William P. Revels

duce her. Henry Berry generally warned such suitors away. He told one white man, "You are taking advantage of my circumstances and absence to be familiar with my family. Now, you better pack up and get out of this county." The man reportedly lost no time in doing as ordered; by reputation Lowrie warned only once. Whatever the relationship between Rhoda and her husband might have been, she always remembered him as "the handsomest man I ever saw."

As a result of his jailbreak, sheriffs throughout the North Carolina-South Carolina border area were instructed to arrest Lowrie on sight, if they could find him. This proved impossible to do, since he took refuge in the swamps, where he was soon joined by other members of his band. Although some men came and went, the most constant members of the "Lowrie Gang" were

Henry Berry and two of his older brothers, Steve and Tom; two cousins, Calvin and Henderson Oxendine; two friends who were also his brothers-in-law, Andrew and Boss Strong; and two other Indians, John Dial and William Chavis. In addition, there were two black members, George Applewhite and Eli Ewin, the latter better known as "Shoemaker John"; and one white member, Zachariah T. McLauchlin, thus making one of North Carolina's first integrated bands. It was a strange group in many ways, but all were animated by at least one common factor: They had all felt the sting of injustice at one time or another and in one way or another.

Among the Indian members of the guerrilla band, Steve Lowrie was the eldest, and was also considered the most violent and hot-tempered. Although only five feet, ten inches tall, he was powerfully built and menacing in appearance with his thick black, straight hair, his thin, short mustache, and his penetrating eyes. He reputedly took part in most, if not all of the killings and robberies attributed to the Lowrie band. By contrast, Tom Lowrie was temperate in mood, preferring to avoid bloodshed when possible. Darker-skinned than his brother, he fought out of a sense of duty, having little appetite for some of the violent activities of the band. The two Oxendines took up their guns largely because of their relationship to the Lowries and because a kinsman, Hector Oxendine, had been slain by whites, and no attempts had been made to capture and punish his murderers. At the time he joined the band in 1866, Boss Strong was just fourteen years old, but he quickly became Henry Berry Lowrie's closest friend and most trusted subordinate. Apparently Andrew Strong, a powerfully built six-footer, didn't join the gang until 1870. Although he was labeled "the Oily Gammon of the party" because of his innocent, injured looks and his soft manner of speech ("the honey will drop from his tongue almost into the wound he inflicts," said one observer), there were nevertheless times when he urged compassion toward intended gang victims. Like Boss Strong, John Dial, an apprentice blacksmith, was only fourteen when he joined the band, but like the Lowries he had seen his family threatened and harassed by the local authorities. His father was George Dial, who had been arrested at the same time as Allen and William Lowrie and who, shortly after their deaths, was forced by the Home Guard to participate in a search for camps used by Union escapees. This young Indian, instantly recognizable by the presence of a marble-sized wart on the left side of his nose, later lost favor with his people by turning state's evidence against other members of the band. The last Lumbee to follow Henry Berry Lowrie's leadership was William Chavis, a tall, bright, fine looking man of about thirty years, whose chief function was to make bullets for his comrades. As soon as he was declared an outlaw by the civil authorities, as eventually happened to all band members, Chavis left Robeson County and was never again seen in the area.

The two Negro members of the Lowrie band, George Applewhite and "Shoemaker John," were ex-slaves and skilled artisans. The former was a mason and plasterer; the latter, as his nickname indicates, was a shoemaker. In many ways Applewhite was the "lucky" member of the band. On two separate occasions he was

The stretch of seaboard coastline track which passes through Moss Neck extends for 78.86 miles without a curve, making it the longest straight stretch of railroad track in the United States. In the mid-nineteenth century the Moss Neck station, which no longer stands, was a center of Lumbee activity.

—*Photo by William P. Revels*

shot, once in the thigh and a second time in the back of the head. Following each incident he was reported dead. But Applewhite, to the chagrin of his pursuers, always survived; on one occasion he kept himself alive for days, eating only watermelon and other fruits. "Shoemaker John" took part in several raids staged by the band in 1869, but like John Dial, he would turn state's evidence in an attempt to save himself.

The only white member of the Lowrie gang was Zack McLauchlin, a youth of Scottish descent who apparently became an active member of the band in 1870, though he had long been associated with the Scuffletonians. Having grown up in an area where his closest neighbors were Lumbees, he had acquired Indian friends; he took part in Indian social activities, and was attracted to the pretty Indian girls. However, such involvement bred resentment in the white community toward McLauchlin, causing him to become a social outcast and ultimately pushing him into the camp of Henry Berry Lowrie.

In the months that followed, the Lowrie band engaged in numerous raids "in retaliation" for past injustices, but no lives were lost or taken during this time. Then, in 1868, in response to a petition from the white citizens of Robeson County, Governor W. W. Holden, a Republican pledged to "law and order," issued a proclamation which outlawed Henry Berry and his followers. In an attempt to restore order by peaceful means, a meeting was arranged between Benjamin A. Howell, the sheriff of Robeson County, Dr. Alfred Thomas, the local agent of the Freedmen's Bureau, and Henry Berry Lowrie. At the meeting, which occurred at Lowrie's house, the white visitors were served a "sumptuous repast" and Henry Berry then entertained them with his considerable talents as a fiddler. The purpose of the meeting was to convince Lowrie to give himself up, and to take a chance with the new system of Republican courts. It was argued that he would at least have a chance for a fair trial. Henry Berry agreed to the proposal on condition that he would be assured of good treatment and security.

When the trio reached Lumberton, Lowrie was housed in the new county jail and given the treatment he was promised. However, his presence and the fact that he wasn't shackled and put on hard fare upset many white Robesonians. There were threats to take him from his cell and drown him in the river. As rumors circulated and grew uglier, Henry Berry himself caught wind of them and realized the ugly mood that prevailed. Consequently, on December 12, 1868, when the jailor brought him his evening meal, Lowrie confronted him with a knife and a cocked revolver and said, "Look here, I'm tired of this. Open that door and stand aside. If you leave this place for fifteen minutes, you will be shot as you come out." He then walked out of the jail, took cover along the river bank, stopped at a house and helped himself to some crackers, and crossed the bridge leading out of Lumberton. For the second time Henry Berry Lowrie had been in the hands of the law, and for the second time he had escaped. He was never again jailed, nor did he intend to be. He later expressed his feelings about the future when he said: "My band is big enough . . . They are all true men and I could not be as safe with more. We mean to live as long as we can, to kill anybody who hunts us, from the sheriff down, and at last, if we must die, to die game."

One of the Robesonians who incurred the wrath of the Lowrie band was Sheriff Reuben King. Although the Republican candidate, Benjamin Howell, had been proclaimed the winner of the sheriff's office in 1868, most white citizens considered the election fraudulent and continued to look upon King as the real sheriff. Regardless of the political situation, King had earlier made threats against the Indian band; but worse, he had a reputation for overzealous enforcement of the laws against Robeson's minority peoples. Thus, Henry Berry and his followers determined to rob King, reputedly a wealthy man who kept much money at his home. In planning the robbery, John Dial prophetically noted "The old Sheriff may resist us," to which Boss Strong replied, "If he does, we'll kill him."

On Saturday night, January 23, 1869, the Lowrie band appeared at the sheriff's home and walked in virtually unnoticed. King and a neighbor, S. E. Ward, were talking together, when Henry Berry's presence was felt. King looked at the outlaw, who demanded his money, and then he foolishly lunged for Lowrie's gun. In the scuffle the gun was fired into the floor. However, standing in the shadows was George Applewhite. He fired his revolver, striking King in the back. At the same time, John Dial fired at Ward, wounding him severely. As the sheriff lay mortally wounded, he called out, "Water, I am burning up! For God's sake give me water!" One member of the band replied harshly to his request with "God damn you, what did you fight for." While the group did find one hundred and fifty-five dollars in currency, and twenty dollars in gold, Henry Berry was always ashamed of this incident, for he had not wanted King to be killed.

The murder of Reuben King led to a concerted effort to capture the Lowrie band, and at the same time marked a change in the attitude of Henry Berry and his followers toward killing. Whereas the band was earlier determined to slay only those men responsible for the death of Allen and William Lowrie, now, for reasons of self-preservation, they would also kill their main pursuers. For the next five years, death was a familiar figure in Robeson County.

The leader of the forces attempting the capture of the Lowrie band in 1869 was Owen Clinton Norment, known as "Black Owen" because of his dark eyes, black hair and beard. A member of one of Robeson's old-line families, Norment saw in cooperation with the Republican regime an opportunity to recover lost influence. Therefore, he accepted the position of Captain of the Police Guard and diligently hunted the Indian outlaws. By the fall of 1869, Norment's campaign against the Lowries was bearing fruit. He managed to capture eight men—six Indians and two blacks—who were considered important followers of the Indian guerrilla leader, and two—"Shoemaker John" and John Dial—were persuaded, probably with a combination of threats and bribes, to cooperate with the authorities. The trial of the eight men was scheduled for the spring term of the Robeson County Superior Court; it promised to be a sensational event. But even more important, 1870 was the first of three years of absolute terror in southeastern North Carolina. During this period at least eighteen people—pursuers, outlaws, and innocents alike—died in the Lowrie War. The anger and frustrations of a generation, stirred in a cauldron of hatred, now yielded a bitter brew, the aftertaste of which would be present for years to come.

Notably, however, through all of these events, Henry Berry and Boss Strong remained free, and raids continued in Robeson with the help of lesser known allies. On March 19, 1870, two weeks before the trials were to begin, Lowrie and several followers went to the home of Captain Norment to seek retribution. It was early evening, a time when Norment told stories to his children before sending them to bed. After the children were asleep and while sitting with his wife, the militia officer remarked that he heard a noise. In a few moments he arose, opened the door, and stepped out, leaving it open. His wife recalled looking out and seeing the "flash of a gun" and hearing her husband groan at the same time. "She caught him and pulled him inside the house. He whispered to her to close and fasten the door, and hand him his rifle. . ." She did as told and then propped him up, using her own body for support so both his hands would be free should he have to use his gun.

Aroused by the noise, members of the household went for a doctor to help the severely wounded man. A Dr. Dick was found, but as he approached the vicinity of the Norment Plantation, a man stepped out of the darkness and shot the mule pulling his buggy. The doctor and several men accompanying him jumped from the buggy and covered the last mile of their trip on foot. Unfortunately, in his fright, Dr. Dick left his bag with its instruments and medicines in the abandoned buggy. Several Negro servants went to recover the doctor's bag, but help came too late for "Black Owen." He died the following morning.

On April 1, 1870, George Applewhite and Stephen Lowrie became the first members of the band to be tried for the murder of Reuben King. Because of the tension in Lumberton, their trial was moved to Whiteville. The evidence against them was supplied by John Dial, though he said when testifying that his earlier confession had been extracted by force and promises and was untrue. Despite this retraction, the two defendants were convicted and sentenced to die by hanging. In the meantime, other members of the band being held in Lumberton managed to escape with the help of a woman, probably Rhoda Strong Lowrie, who brought them an auger. One of the escapees was "Shoemaker John," who had turned state's evidence and now disappeared from the scene.

All of the remaining members of the band who were still in the hands of the authorities were transferred to the Wilmington jail, where Calvin and Henderson Oxendine were already incarcerated. This structure was solid brick and had a maximum-security cell in which the Indian prisoners were placed. However, again the band members were able to get tools and make their escape. A Lumbee tale says that Rhoda Lowrie walked the eighty miles from Scuffletown to Wilmington, went to the jail, and there created a diversion with her womanly charms, thus allowing an aide to tie tools to a string with which the outlaws were able to draw the tools into their cell. With the exception of Calvin Oxendine, who declared he was innocent of the crime with which he was charged and declined to leave, all of the band members slipped out of the jail in the early morning hours of June 13. Following this last incredible jailbreak, the outlaws took a month to make their way back to the swamps of Robeson. Traveling through the wilderness was difficult and they used extreme caution, not wanting to risk recapture.

By 1870 Henry Berry Lowrie had become the most hunted and feared man in North Carolina's history. The state legislature would ultimately place a $12,000 bounty on his head, and $6,000 each on the heads of Steve and Tom Lowrie, Boss Strong, Henderson Oxendine, and George Applewhite. The reward for Andrew Strong was only $5,000, since he was relatively a newcomer to the band. In addition to the rewards offered by the state, the Robeson County commissioners offered a purse of several hundred dollars. All of the rewards carried the provision "dead or alive," and the tempo of violence picked up in Robeson County.

After the Wilmington escape, the band was reconstituted and resumed its raids. One of the uglier episodes involving the Indian band began on October 3, 1870, and concerned a distillery operated by one Angus Leach. The band appeared at Leach's place and began to take large quantities of brandy. When he protested, he was struck on the hip with a gun stock. A Negro who attempted to help the old man was whipped with a wagon trace and his ears slit with a penknife. The next day some of Leach's neighbors who had left their fruit with him for distillation started in pursuit of the outlaws. They discovered them at George Applewhite's home between Plummer's Station and Red Banks. A battle began and the band retreated into Long Swamp. The posse pursued them, and before the day was over Applewhite, Boss Strong, and Henderson Oxendine were wounded. A white youth, Stephen Davis, in attempting to force the fight in the edge of a field, lay dead. Knowing that several of the band were wounded and believing they could trap the Lowries in the swamp, more than one hundred and fifty men took up positions around it. Because the authorities still feared pursuing the band into the swamp itself, the sheriff, Roderick McMillan, who had been a member of the company of Home Guard that executed Allen and William Lowrie, appealed for a battery of artillery to use against the outlaws. The artillery was sent, but arrived too late. Word came that the Lowrie band had been sighted ten miles from the swamp. The guerrillas were as good at slipping traps as they were at getting out of jails.

GUERRILLA WAR

The authorities, frustrated in their attempts to take Henry Berry and his followers, turned their wrath on some of the Indians they believed were supplying the outlaws with food, weapons, and information. Andrew Strong and Malcolm (Make) Sanderson were two of those who fell into this category. Strong had kinship ties with the band and had himself been implicated in the King murder by John Dial, though the evidence against him was weak and it appears he had taken no part in the group's activities prior to 1870. Indeed, he was known as a hardworking logger who only managed to live from day to day. Yet, on the night of October 5, 1870, he was awakened by twenty armed men, who told him to get dressed and come with them. When he came out, Strong was surprised to see Make Sanderson, an Indian, with the group. As they moved down the road, one of the men said to Andrew, "You'll never see morning again." When he asked why, the response came that ". . . you are a damn nigger and a spy for the Lowries and so was Sanderson." They had determined to kill them all.

The two captives were bound together with a plow line and eventually taken to William C. McNeill's mill pond. Although the captain of the Police Guard was Murdock McLean, apparently the real authority was John Taylor, a rich planter, a member of the wartime Home Guard, and a known racist. The two men asked for mercy but Taylor had none. His reply to their plea was, "If all the mulatto (Indian) blood in the country was in you two and a movement of my foot would send you to hell, I would make it." When the militiamen began to prepare for the execution of the two Indians, Sanderson asked for time to pray, which was granted. While he made peace with God, Strong worked to free himself from his ropes, succeeded, and fled into Bear Swamp amidst a hail of buckshot and ball. Sanderson was executed as planned. His body was thrown into the mill race. Strong, on the other hand, became the newest member of the outlaw band.

It quickly became known among the Indian community that John Taylor was responsible for the death of Sanderson. Taylor knew his life was in danger now, unless he could somehow placate the Indian people. To accomplish this, he began negotiations with the Sanderson family, offering money as compensation for the death of their kinsman. When it became clear that the family wanted justice, Taylor began preparations to leave the area. It took time, however, to dispose of his property. He would no doubt have moved more quickly, had he known of Henry Berry Lowrie's vow to kill him if the legal authorities took no action.

While Lowrie watched Taylor and bided his time, tragedy struck a member of the gang. Zack McLauchlin, following a night of carousing and drinking in the company of another white youth, apparently tried to convince or force his companion, Henry Biggs, to join the Lowrie group. McLauchlin told Biggs, "I'll kill you right here unless you join with me and rob the smoke houses and shanties of some of these freedmen. We want you with our crowd and you've got to come or die." Biggs said later that he knew he had to escape from McLauchlin or kill him. In a drunken stupor, McLauchlin insisted they stop for the night in a swamp. Not fully trusting Biggs, the outlaw youth made him sleep in the light of the fire where he could see him. The liquor had a drugging effect, however, and McLauchlin was soon in a deep sleep, from which he would not arise. Biggs pulled a pistol from the sheath in Mc-Lauchlin's belt and fired two shots into his body. He went to Lumberton, reported the killing, located the body for the authorities, collected four hundred dollars' reward, and left the county. Attrition now began to take its toll of the Lowrie band.

Less than two weeks after the murder of Zack McLauchlin, Robeson County was rocked by the even more brutal murder of John Saunders, an undercover agent trying to get the Lowrie band out of the area, or to trap them for the authorities. A Boston detective, Saunders was apparently recruited for this dangerous assignment by the sheriff of New Hanover County, who saw an opportunity for quick wealth in the bounties offered for the Lowrie band, wealth he would share with the agent if he survived. Arriving in Robeson County in 1869, Saunders settled in Scuffle-town as a teacher, believing that this role would win the confidence of the Lumbees. In time, he made contact with Henry Berry Lowrie and told him he would help the band escape the area for the frontier or even Mexico. Saunders apparently planned to have them taken prisoner in South Carolina or Georgia, something he believed would be easier to do at a distance from Robeson County with its many sympathetic people and friendly swamps.

While Saunders' plan appeared to be foolproof, suspicion born of years of danger caused Henry Berry and his group to watch the outsider carefully. As they studied his movements, they eventually learned that he had contacts with the William C. Mc-Neill family, into which the hated John Taylor had married. Henry Berry quickly deduced that this family wasn't going to help him escape, and he now planned the execution of Saunders, the man who obviously intended to betray him to his enemies. The outlaws were supposed to come to a camp which Saunders had established near Moss Neck, on November 19, 1870, for the "migration" out of North Carolina. When they failed to show up, he called a meeting with the McNeill boys for Sunday afternoon at the camp. The next day one of the McNeills arrived late and was greeted with the news that "they were all surrounded, to move would be certain death, covered as they all were, by the shotguns and pistols of their besiegers." When the young McNeill made a move for his pistol, four men rose up in the bushes close beside him, including the Indian leader.

The night was filled with uncertainty for the McNeills, particularly after Henry Berry told Malcolm McNeill: "God damn your soul, I want you to tell me where Saunders is. He is expected here. If you don't tell me where he is and why he doesn't come, I will kill you dead. I intend to kill you anyhow when I get Saunders. You had better own right up." McNeill gave no information, and Henry Berry took no action, apparently intending only to frighten him.

The next morning, Steve Lowrie was standing watch. He captured John Saunders as he approached the camp. The band decided to take Saunders to their base in Back Swamp, called the Devil's Den, and to release the McNeill boys. However, before they were allowed to leave, Henry Berry told the most defiant one:

> God damn you, I have a great mind to kill you right here. I ought to have killed you before. You have been hunting me for years. You are young, stout and healthy; however, I don't want to take your blood. I hate to interfere with you and your people; but you have already done so much to have me hanged or shot that it would be right if I should kill you right here. I will let you go this time, however; but you make yourself scarce in this country. Your folks may keep the shebang at Moss Neck; but you won't know when your time has come. Get out of this country mighty quick. Your father may stay here if he wants to but tell him to walk a chalk line.

Once they reached the Devil's Den, the outlaws debated Saunders' fate. Andrew Strong and Tom Lowrie were opposed to killing him, and pleaded for his life. Strong, remembering his brush with death and the murder of Make Sanderson, said, "God knows I pity you for I have been in the very presence of death myself and I can understand your feelings." But Henry Berry and Steve Lowrie were for killing him and they swung the balance to their side. While the outlaws argued among themselves, Saunders seized a knife and attempted to commit suicide by cutting one of his wrists, but the cut wasn't deep enough.

In the end, Saunders waited three days for death. He was allowed to take a pill the outlaws thought was arsenic, but it had no real effect. Finally, on Thursday, November 24, 1870, the outlaws told Saunders his time to die had come. He was allowed to write a letter to his wife in Boston; then he was blindfolded and tied to a tree. Tom Lowrie could not bear to watch the execution, and left until it was over. The other members of the band drew lots, to determine who would shoot the prisoner; Steve Lowrie won. Without further delay he stepped up and emptied both barrels of his shotgun in the Bostonian's face. Andrew Strong buried Saunders as "decently as he could" and saw to it that his last letter to his wife was sent. Henry Berry later justified the murder of the detective with the comment, "The efficiency and morale of my company compelled me to kill Saunders. We all pitied him but if I hadn't killed him I would have had no right to kill John Taylor or any of the rest."

The outlaw leader, who was a man of his word, had not forgotten his promise to kill John Taylor. On January 14, 1871, Henry Berry, accompanied by Boss Strong, rose from the side of the road, two hundred yards from a company of soldiers encamped at Moss Neck Station sent into the area for maintaining order, one hundred yards from where Make Sanderson was killed in the autumn, "at a distance of less than ten yards, shot the top of John Taylor's head off," as he passed through the area. "Fragments of the brain fell into the mill pond and floated down against the bank with the current," according to one account. Lowrie ran to the "quivering body" of Taylor, robbed it of fifty dollars, and, along with his comrade, disappeared into the swamp as the troops came down from the depot. The local whites were shocked and demands that Lowrie and his men be caught or killed increased.

From February through April, 1871, three men were killed and one Lowrie band member executed. The first man killed was Benjamin Bethea, a black radical murdered either because of his politics or because he refused to help a posse in their search for the Lowrie people. Then later, a posse surrounded Henry Berry

Lowrie and his group at the guerrilla leader's home, while he was visiting his family. A fight ensued, and believing the band was trapped, the sheriff went for additional men. The outlaws, however, escaped through a trap door that led into a tunnel and lay in wait for their pursuers. In the battle that followed, Roderick Thompson and young Giles Inman were slain. Henry Berry always regretted Inman's death and later told the youth's father that he was sorry that he had killed his son Giles. But the most notable development of this period was the capture of Henderson Oxendine, his trial and conviction for the 1870 murder of Stephen Davis, and his execution by hanging.

Henderson Oxendine was arrested at the house of George Applewhite, where he was visiting, and taken to Lumberton for trial. The verdict of guilty was expected and he knew there was little hope for escape. Ironically, during the same time that Henderson was being tried and held for execution, his brother Calvin, after two years in the Wilmington jail, was being tried in Southport, for the 1869 slaying of Sheriff King. With the help of a Methodist minister, Henderson wrote Calvin a letter, in which he said, "you know what it is to be deprived of your liberty, but you have never known the agony I have endured for the past few days." However, Calvin's ordeal would end happily. He was able to prove that he was working, away from the county, when King was killed, and to muster a number of character witnesses. When the case went to the jury, the verdict was for acquittal.

Henderson Oxendine's mother came to the jail to be with her son on March 17, 1871, the day of execution. A multitude gathered to watch the hanging and to see how a member of the Lowrie gang would die. Henderson Oxendine faced the end with courage. He ascended the scaffold, opened a hymnal, and sang the song commencing, "And shall I yet delay," followed by "Amazing Grace! How sweet the Sound." He prayed softly for a moment and then with pride and stoicism stood calmly while the black hood was drawn over his face. At precisely 12:30 p.m. the trap fell, and Henderson Oxendine became the only member of the Lowrie gang to be executed publicly. There were no attempts at rescue.

The capture and execution of Henderson Oxendine inspired

the Police Guard, causing them to increase their efforts to drive away or capture the Lowrie band. Indeed, the authorities now resorted to the tactic of arresting the wives of several members of the gang, including Rhoda Lowrie, and holding them as hostages in the belief that this would draw the Indian guerillas out into the open. To give this tactic an air of legality, the women were to be charged with "aiding and abetting" the outlaws.

In the midst of the militia's seizure of the outlaws' wives, a unit of eighteen men, commanded by Captain Charles McRae, had an unusual and surprising confrontation with Henry Berry Lowrie.[7] While resting at Wiregrass Landing on the banks of the Lumbee River near Harper's Ferry, the soldiers heard the soft sounds of a boat and looked up to see the Indian leader paddling a small, flat bottomed scow, his belt of arms unbuckled and laying in the bottom of the boat. Instantly the whole party opened fire. Lowrie threw himself into the dark waters of the Lumbee River, off the side of his scow opposite his attackers, tilted the boat for protection, reached inside for his weapons, and resolutely advanced toward the militiamen, aiming and firing as coolly as if he were at the head of his band on solid ground. The boldness of this move and the accuracy of Lowrie's fire panicked his attackers, causing them to flee from their positions. While the militia carried two wounded men away with them, the Indian leader escaped unharmed. The fight at Wiregrass Landing added greatly to Lowrie's reputation as a marksman and warrior. It is from such events that legends grow.

If the authorities believed that the arrest of the outlaws' wives would serve their purposes, they soon learned that intimidation was a poor weapon. Rather than responding in an emotional and rash fashion, as the Police Guard expected, Henry Berry Lowrie allowed several days to pass before he even acknowledged that the women were captives. The interim between the arrest of the Indian women and Lowrie's response filled Lumberton with an air of excitement which, with the passage of time,

---

7. The actual number of men in the company is not known, ranging from a reported number of ten to twenty-three. W. McKee Evans, who has made the most intensive examination of the band's activities, accepts the figure of eighteen and the authors of this book are guided on this point by his scholarship.

gave way to a mood of tension. When Lowrie finally revealed what he intended to do, it was not to surrender.

On July 14, 1871, Henry Berry, accompanied by his brother Steve and the two Strongs, went to the home of John McNair. Upon arrival, the group told McNair they had come for breakfast and a meal was prepared and served to them. When they had finished eating, Henry Berry told his somewhat shaken host,

> Mr. McNair, I want you to gear up and go to Lumberton, where they have put my wife in jail for no crime but because she is my wife; that ain't her fault, and they can't make it so. You people won't let me work to get my living, and I have got to take it from you; but, God knows, she'd like to see me make my own bread. You go to Lumberton and tell the Sheriff and County Commissioners that if they don't let her out of that jail I'll retaliate on the white women of Burnt Swamp Township. Some of them shall come to the swamp with me if she is kept in jail, because they can't get me.

Lowrie then dictated the message he wanted McNair to carry to the authorities in Lumberton. The note said:

> We make a request that our wives who were arrested a few days ago, and placed in jail, be released to come home to their families by Monday morning, and if not, the Bloodiest times will be here that ever was before—the life of every man will be in jeopardy.[8]

HENRY B. LOWRIE
STEPHEN LOWRIE
ANDREW STRONG
BOSS STRONG

Although the authorities, civil and military, resolved to stand firm in the face of Lowrie's ultimatum, most of the county's white citizens were fearful that the outlaws would carry out their threats. After several days of hesitation, the civil authorities surrendered to public pressure and released the wives of the band members. They returned by train to the Red Banks station on the very day the ultimatum was to expire. All of Robeson County breathed a sigh of relief.

---

8. Another version of the note had Henry Berry Lowrie saying that if the women weren't released by a stated time, he would "drench the county in blood and ashes." Regardless of the variations in language, the intent of the message was the same.

Stewartsville Cemetery. This cemetery was founded in 1785, incorporated in 1913, and restored in 1965. It uniquely reflects the tri-racial situation that exists in southeastern North Carolina, having distinctly white, Indian, and black sections. The first Indian was buried in Stewartsville during the Civil War era. The cemetery is located fifteen miles east of Pembroke in Scotland County, North Carolina.

But if a holocaust had been averted, the determination of the militia to capture or kill the Lowrie band remained. The determination of the outlaws to survive also persisted. One of the more energetic of the young militia officers was Captain Murdock McLean. He had taken part in the Home Guard's execution of Allen and William Lowrie and in the Police Guard's execution of Make Sanderson. Thus, he was one of the men against whom Henry Berry Lowrie had sworn vengeance. Lowrie's anger had been heightened by the militia's part in the arrest of his wife, and so, in mid-July, 1871, he struck back. As Murdock McLean, his brother Hugh, and a friend, Archy McCallum, who was also a participant in the anti-Lowrie operations, rode in a buggy toward Shoe Heel, Henry Berry Lowrie rose from a "blind" at roadside and fired his shotgun at the three men. The McLean brothers were mortally wounded, but McCallum jumped from the buggy and made his way to Shoe Heel, having suffered only a flesh wound in one leg. While most Robesonians could understand why Henry Berry wanted to kill Murdock McLean (both had long been bitter enemies), the younger Hugh was one of the innocents of the Lowrie War. Yet, his death was not totally without purpose; it accelerated a desire to end hostilities between the whites and Indians quickly, and by any means.

By late summer, 1871, most Robesonians agreed that efforts should be made to reach an accord with Lowrie and his followers, even to the extent of allowing them to leave the area unharmed. Although the adjutant-general of North Carolina, John C. Gorman, was in the vicinity with a detachment of United States troops, the horrors of the struggle had dragged on too long, and most local people were not interested in continuing efforts to destroy the band by military force. Consequently, Gorman agreed to meet with the outlaws to see if some end to the conflict could be reached. Both sides pledged their good behavior. Gorman later described the meeting.

> While one desperado picketed the road and scouted the vicinity as an assurance against surprise and betrayal, the others bid [me] be seated on a log near the roadside, ranged themselves around him, and opened the conference through their

leader by thanking me for consenting to meet them. He [Henry Berry Lowrie] then gave his version of their grievances, and attempted to justify themselves for the course they had pursued and acts committed, and in conclusion desired to ascertain whether, in the event of their surrender, I could not stipulate and agree that they might harmlessly go, or be sent to the Indian Territory, or to some other remote part of the public domain, as has since been done by the Federal government with. . . other Indian malefactors.

Gorman further stated that Lowrie denied responsibility for some of the murders attributed to him and his band, and insisted that the ones they had committed were justified. The adjutant-general noted that all members of the gang were in the "prime of young manhood, and apparently in the best of health," that they were dressed in homespun, and "formidably armed." Henry Berry carried a "Spencer rifle, a double-barreled shotgun, two revolvers, and a bowie knife; each of his men carried a double-barreled shotgun apiece and several revolvers."

The meeting lasted for two hours, and when it came to an end, Gorman asked Lowrie why he didn't simply leave the state. Henry Berry replied, "Robeson County is the only land I know. I can hardly read, and do not know where to go if I leave these woods and swamps, where I was raised. If I can get safe conduct and pardon I will go anywhere. . . But these people will not let me live and I do not mean to enter any jail again." Gorman was moved by their plight, but told Lowrie he lacked the authority to grant the terms he sought. Interestingly, several other meetings followed. During the weeks of talk the outlaws conducted themselves as peacefully as the circumstances allowed. Yet, in the end, Gorman and the federal troops were withdrawn for "lack of progress." Whether there was any progress is uncertain to this day, as will be shown.

Shortly after Gorman and the federal troops withdrew, the state legislature increased the reward for the outlaws; bounty hunters became more abundant and aggressive than ever, and the Indian guerrillas retaliated in their own way. In one of their most audacious moves, the Lowrie band, in the early morning hours of February 16, 1872, staged a raid on Lumberton. They stole an iron safe from the store of some prominent merchants, Pope and McLeod, which reportedly contained much of the town's money (there was no bank), and then, to add insult to injury, they stole the iron safe from the sheriff's office. The combined weight of the safes proved too great for the cart they were using and so they left the sheriff's safe in the middle of a Lumberton street. This was the most lucrative raid the band ever made, for the safe contained twenty-two thousand dollars. However, the significance of this robbery was not in its success or amount of proceeds, but rather in the fact that Henry Berry Lowrie mysteriously disappeared shortly afterwards. The last two years of the Lowrie war is largely a tale of bounty hunters and methodical pursuit.

One of the first successful bounty hunters was James "Donahoe" McQueen, who resided in upper Robeson County. This hunter was the illegitimate son of a Scottish father and an Indian mother. He knew the ways of the men he pursued. McQueen set out to kill the Strong brothers and in early March 1872, he staked out Andrew Strong's house in Back Swamp and patiently awaited the appearance of his quarry. He was not disappointed. Concerning his experience there McQueen later said:

I fixed a good blind about one hundred and fifty yards from the house, and lying down I watched the rest of the night and all the next day, eating some provisions I had brought along. About half-past seven p.m., Friday, Andrew Strong came out of the woods, and after stopping and looking in all directions, he went into the house, and directly came out and gave a low call, when Boss came out of the woods to the house. They were each armed with rifles and two or three revolvers. A little after eight o'clock, when I thought they would be at supper, I slipped up to the house and looked in through the cat hole in the door. As I supposed they were eating their supper by the light of the hearth. . . I kept watching until Boss laid down on the floor with his feet to the fire and his head towards me, and commenced playing on a mouth harp; then I saw my chance, and I pushed my rifle through the cat-hole in the door until it was not over three or four feet from his head, and took steady aim and shot. When I fired the women in the house screamed and said 'he's shot.'

Those inside the house extinguished the fire as soon as the shooting occurred. McQueen hid in the shadows for a short time, hoping for a shot at Andrew Strong. Sensing danger to himself, however, he soon left and returned to Shoe Heel. He returned the next morning with a posse and found the women at the house scrubbing up blood on the floor where Boss had been lying when shot. When questioned, the women said that during the night Andrew Strong went out and got Steve Lowrie and the two carried off Boss, but that they didn't know where. Because of the element of uncertainty concerning Boss's death (some said he was not dead, only severely wounded), McQueen had to wait a year before the state legislature finally awarded him the six thousand dollar bounty on the outlaw's head. Boss Strong's body was never found.

Throughout the spring of 1872, Col. Francis M. Wishart, now heading the militia, continued his efforts to round up the Lowrie band. In May, 1872, only Tom Lowrie, Steve Lowrie, and Andrew Strong remained in the area, all the others had been killed or had disappeared. On May 2, Col. Wishart met Steven and Andrew at Moss Neck, the site of a railroad station and turpentine distillery about ten miles from Lumberton. Wishart and Lowrie talked briefly of a possible compromise. Before separating, they agreed to meet again, unarmed, to talk over their differences.

A few days later, Steve Lowrie sent word to Col. Wishart to meet him near the Lebanon Presbyterian Church, located about two miles from the Red Banks station. Wishart agreed to go; he hoped to convince the outlaws to leave the area. Steve Lowrie, by reputation "the craftiest and most blood-thirsty" of the guerrillas, fearing a trap, had Andrew Strong go to the meeting place, where he concealed himself in case help was needed. According to belief among the Lumbees, the two enemies met as planned. They talked for a time and finally decided to separate. Then, as reported by Clifton Oxendine, a Lumbee historian, "As Steve turned to go, Wishart drew a revolver, which he had concealed, and shot at him. At this point, Andrew Strong shot Wishart. . ." Whether Wishart was the originator or the victim of duplicity remains debatable.

Wishart's death led to renewed efforts to catch or kill the surviving Indian guerrillas. The colonel's younger brother Aladon Strong Wishart, and a half-brother, Robert Evander Wishart, took the lead in reorganizing the so-called Wishart Company for yet another manhunt. This company learned that Tom Lowrie was planning to attend a political meeting in the Burnt Swamp community. Along the trail from the Indian's home, they built a blind for cover, and awaited his appearance. In the early morning hours of July 20, 1872, the militiamen endured the biting mosquitoes as they anticipated success. About eight o'clock they heard voices. It was Tom and a friend arguing about whether it was safe for him to attend a public rally. As they talked, the whites from their hidden position opened fire on Lowrie. Both men turned and fled, but Lowrie had been hit, and collapsed after running about one hundred yards. When the militiamen approached him, Lowrie tried to bring up his weapon to fire on them, but he was too weak. He died shortly afterwards, holding to his Spencer rifle so tightly that "the party had to loosen the fingers, one by one, by main force." Lowrie's body was carried to Lumberton, where his hunters were paid $6,200 in state and county bounties. The slain man's funeral was preached the next afternoon at New Hope Church near Pates. Most Scuffletonians, many of them armed, turned out to pay their last respects to a member of the Lowrie band, one whom they viewed as a neighbor and friend.

With the death of Tom Lowrie, the band was reduced to two members, Andrew Strong and Steve Lowrie. Although these two men could no longer threaten the white communities, they continued to roam freely through the swamplands and to serve as reminders of Indian resistance. The rewards on their heads, however, insured continued pursuit among those with visions of quick wealth. On Christmas day, 1872, Strong and Lowrie went to John Humphrey's store at Pate's to warn William Wilson, a white man clerking there, that he had been talking about them in a way they did not like, and demanded that he cease. Wilson said little, and Strong became angry, telling the clerk he would give him until train time the next day to pack up and leave the county. Strong concluded the conversation with a vow to kill him if he failed to go.

Since it was a holiday, Strong and Lowrie left to take part in a Christmas frolic. After their departure, Wilson loaded his double barrelled shotgun with buckshot and concealed it in case his intimidators returned. Late in the afternoon, Strong came back alone. After making some purchases, he walked out on the porch, carelessly laid his gun down, and leaned against the post with his back to the interior of the store. Wilson saw his chance to kill an enemy and get a large reward. He removed his weapon, slipped up behind Strong and shot him in the back of the neck. Strong died instantly. Wilson, hovering over his victim, ordered several Indians who were present to get a wagon and mules and carry him and Strong's body to Lumberton. The clerk collected the bounty and left the area.

At the beginning of 1873, Steve Lowrie was the only member of the band still active in Robeson County. Throughout the year, the bounty hunters tracked him, but he always succeeded in escaping. It was a lonely, desperate year for this man who knew the danger of roaming too far from the swamps. The constant tension of his solitary and precarious existence began to wear Steve down. He grew pale and thin, and began to drink too much and too regularly. His hopes for a pardon virtually disappeared when the Amnesty Act of 1873, passed to absolve members of semi-political bands for acts of violence during Reconstruction, specifically exempted him. The last section of the law said, "the provisions of this act shall not be construed to extend amnesty . . . to Steve Lowrie." He is the only individual specifically mentioned in the law, apparently because Henry Berry Lowrie and George Applewhite were presumed to be dead.[9] A later attempt to gain a direct pardon from the governor had no success and Steve must have sensed that he was doomed.

In late February, 1874, a covered whiskey wagon stopped for the night on the John McNair plantation, and country people from all three races gathered for some merrymaking. Steve Lowrie watched the proceedings from the edge of a swamp for awhile, but soon his taste for liquor and music and his need for company,

---

9. Ironically, Applewhite was later found alive, arrested, but finally pardoned under the Amnesty Act of 1873. He lived out his life plying his trade as a mason.

brought him to the camp. As the night passed, Steve became careless and agreed to play a song on the banjo. He handed his rifle to a Negro boy, bowed his head to tune the instrument; and then straightened up and began to play, totally unaware that three bounty hunters had been tracking him and were waiting for just such a moment. Two of them fired on him simultaneously; the third man rushed up and assured his death with an ax. The next day his body was carried to Lumberton and claim was made for the reward. The Lowrie War was over and an uneasy peace returned to Robeson County for the first time in a decade.

THE MYSTERY OF HENRY BERRY LOWRIE

More than one hundred years after the Lowrie War, the Indians of Robeson County still ponder and discuss the sudden disappearance of Henry Berry Lowrie in 1872. They wonder whether the guerrilla leader was killed and his body secretly buried, or whether he left the state for a safer and friendlier environment. The only certainty is that no one ever collected the reward placed on his head. The mystery that surrounds him is unlikely ever to be cleared up to the satisfaction of all.

Among those who believe that Henry Berry left the area is his ninety-four year old nephew, Reverend D. F. Lowry. According to Reverend Lowry, Henry Berry and Adjutant-General John C. Gorman became friends as a result of their various meetings in late 1871 and early 1872. Gorman supposedly convinced the guerrilla leader to don a military uniform and take part in the searches for his band, all of which were intentionally futile. Then, when Gorman's mission failed and his troops were ordered out of the area, the adjutant-general agreed to take Henry Berry with him. He had bandages wrapped around the outlaw's face to obscure his identity and spirited him out of Robeson County on the same train that carried his troops. Reverend Lowry said that an aged Indian, Mr. Marcus Dial, told him of the plan to use bandages and that Dial said he was "at the station when the militia were being loaded and a dozen or more had white bandages on," and he had never seen Henry Berry again.

Dr. Earl Lowry, Rev. D. F. Lowry's son, offers a somewhat different and more elaborate version of how Henry Berry escaped from the county. According to Dr. Lowry, Henry Berry faked his death so there would be no pursuers. More specifically, he had the brains of a rabbit scattered about at Steve Lowrie's place, and a dummy filled with straw to deceive the curious. Then, to further confuse his enemies, he had a coffin built for the non-existent corpse and the box bearing the dummy was carried to the area of Harper's Ferry. There the boards were removed and made into a cart, the dummy was unstuffed and the straw thrown into a pond. Thus, no trace of a burial was ever found and no body recovered, because there was nothing to find or recover. Lowry goes on to say that Henry Berry got out of the county by putting on a military uniform and boarding the train as it pulled out at Pates. He concluded his account by saying that his great uncle served for four years in the United States Army and was discharged in Virginia.

A Lumbee tradition says that Henry Berry slipped out of the area in a wooden coffin especially built for that purpose by his friends. According to this story, air holes were drilled in the box, and Lowrie assumed the position of a corpse. It was nailed shut, and placed on a train to carry him away. At some point, he presumably broke out of the coffin and took up residence as a free man in parts unknown.

For every person who says Henry Berry Lowrie left the county, there are equally as many who say he died accidentally in the area of Scuffletown, including, interestingly enough, several others members of the Lowrie family. According to his widow, Mrs. Anna Lowry, Rev. H. H. Lowry believed the guerrilla chieftain accidentally killed himself and was buried in the swamps. Reverend Lowry was one of the founders of the Lumber River Methodist Conference, a son of Calvin, and a brother of the previously-mentioned D. F. Lowry. An even more complete account of Henry Berry's death was provided by Orlin Hayes Lowry, Tom Lowrie's son. Before his death in the mid-twentieth century, Orlin Lowry wrote the following statement, in which he swore that he witnessed his uncle's death.

This tragedy occurred on the morning following the night that the Pope and McLeod safe was robbed. The Lowry gang made their way to Thomas' home, and after arriving there Thomas ordered his wife Frances to prepare Breakfast. While preparing Breakfast all went in the house, except Henry Berry, he remained outside. . . Henry Berry was standing with the breech of his gun resting on the ground, between his feet. Both barrels of his gun exploded, the load taking effect under his chin blowing his brains out. Some of his brains was scattered on the door frame. Thomas calls for a bed sheet to wrap him in, the sheet was hastily gotten, and Henry Berry's body was wraped (sic) therein, and carried away. Thomas gives orders on pain of death to keep Henry's death a secret: the purpose of keeping the death of Henry Berry Lowry a secret was to carry out the desire of Henry Berry Lowry. He told. . . Thomas that he did not want no man to get the reward. . . the State of North Carolina had offered for his body, dead or alive. Therefore his Burial was and is a secret to remain till the Judgment day, so decreed.

Mr. Lowry said in conclusion, "I am the only living eye witness to his death. The other witnesses have passed on to their long home. That which you see with your eyes and hear with your ears, this I affirm.[10]

The belief that Henry Berry accidentally killed himself, apparently while attempting to draw a load from his weapon, is found repeated in a number of places and by many different people. While a few details may vary, the essence of the story is always the same. The *New York Herald*, to illustrate, published an article saying the outlaw accidentally killed himself while hidden in a newly-constructed blind, waiting to see who would come to occupy it. Adjutant-General Gorman, writing in the 1890's, said Lowrie was "accidentally killed by one of his own guns. He had placed it against a corn-crib on his brother Tom's premises, and was reclining on the grass nearby; the gun fell and was discharged, its contents entering the outlaw's head, killing him instantly. He was secretly buried by his comrades. . ."

10. A number of prominent Lumbees say Orlin Lowry told this story many times during his life and that he was always consistent with his account.

While those who believe that Lowrie died may disagree on specific points, most of them accept the same story concerning his burial. It is a widespread belief in the Lumbee community that following Henry Berry's death, a coffin was fashioned by Jesse Oxendine, the body placed in the casket, and it was carried into Back Swamp on a horse-drawn cart. Once they were deep in the swamp, the surviving guerrillas diverted a small stream, dug a grave, lowered the casket into it, covered it with soil, and allowed the stream to resume its natural course. Under the circumstances only the guerrillas ever knew where their leader rested.

The abundance of stories attempting to explain Lowrie's disappearance serve only to heighten the mystery. Some strain the imagination to make them creditable, while others seem to contradict each other. Gorman's account of Lowrie's death seems on the surface to challenge several of the stories stating that the Indian guerrilla left North Carolina. However, if Gorman helped the outlaw escape, as many of his contemporaries believed, to say that Lowrie was killed would be good cover for his own actions and further protection for the Lumbee leader, who was probably still living as the nineteenth century drew to a close. Rhoda Strong Lowrie, who lived out her life in Robeson County, maintained a discreet silence about what she knew or believed had happened to her husband, adding yet another dimension to the mystery. In the final analysis, the situation has become so confused that it is no longer possible to distinguish Henry Berry Lowrie the man, from Henry Berry Lowrie the legend. Perhaps it's not even important to try. As one Lumbee stated, "It doesn't matter how he died, or when he died, or where his body lies for it's dust; it's his spirit that counts."

CONCLUSIONS

Henry Berry Lowrie was known as the "King of Scuffletown." While the name meant lawlessness and terror to the white community, it meant more truly a man who fought oppression, to the Indians. The "King" became a folk hero to his people, a symbol of pride and manhood. Today, in honor of their outlaw-hero, the Lumbees annually give the Henry Berry Lowrie Award to the citizen who best exemplifies the highest standard of service to the community.[11]

Although many Lumbees regret the violence associated with Lowrie and his band, they nevertheless understand that circumstances directed him and his followers onto that path. Henry Berry was, quite simply, a strong man called upon to play a strong man's part in a period which was marred by racial hatred. Many people, whites and blacks as well as Indians, must have supported him, or else he could not have operated for as long a time as he did. While some Indians have asked "What might Lowrie have accomplished if he had lived in a different time?", a more pertinent question might be "What would have happened to the Lumbees in the mid-nineteenth century without this remarkable leader?" The author of *To Die Game*, W. McKee Evans, answers the latter question and summarizes the significance of Lowrie and his band with the following statement:

> The Lowrys clearly made an impact. . . on the home territory of the Lumber River Indians. They appeared on the scene at a particularly difficult period in the history of the Indians. At this time the armed resistance of the plains Indians was being smashed, their numbers decimated, while the Indians of the eastern seaboard had known little but defeat and increasing humiliation for a hundred years. With the triumph of a frankly racist party during Reconstruction, it appeared that nothing could stop the winners from putting the Lumbee River Indians into the same half-free 'place' in which they generally succeeded in putting the blacks. But this effort failed. It appears to have failed, furthermore, to a great extent because of the bold deeds of the Lowrys, which filled the Lumber River Indians with a new pride of race, and a new confidence that despite generations of defeat, revitalized their will to survive as a people.

---

11. The 1974 recipient of the Henry Berry Lowrie Award was Dr. Martin L. Brooks, currently the only practicing Lumbee physician in Robeson County, a man who has served his people with dedication and purpose.

A Prayer for Strength

Oh Father, Whose voice I hear in the winds and
Whose breath gives life to all the world, hear me.
I am a man before You, one of Your many children.
I am small and weak. I need Your strength and
wisdom. Let me walk in beauty, and make my eyes
ever behold the red and purple sunsets. Make my
hands respect the things You have made, my ears
sharp to hear Your voice. Make me wise so that
I may know the things You have taught my people,
the lessons You have hidden in every leaf and
rock. I seek strength, Father, not to be
superior to my brothers, but to be able to fight
my greatest enemy, myself. Make me ever ready
to come to You with clean hands and straight
eyes, so that when life fades as the setting sun,
my spirit may come to You without shame.

—CHIEF TOM WHITE CLOUD
Ojibway Indian

4

Out of Darkness

Although Reconstruction was characterized in Robeson County by the bloodshed and terror of the "Lowrie War," and at the state level by confused politics, the era made one positive contribution to North Carolina's history. Out of a Republican-controlled convention came the Constitution of 1868, a document that remains essentially the organic law of the state. This constitution affected the Indians of Robeson County in two ways. First, it restored a measure of political equality in the state; everyone who met the legal requirements was entitled to vote and hold office. Second, it provided for a public school term of four months for all children, regardless of race. It said nothing about segregated schools. Because of the corruption and confusion of the period, and because there was no separation by races, the public schools foundered, rather than flourished. Not until 1875, when Reconstruction ended at the state level and the Democrats revised the constitution, did North Carolina begin in earnest to establish schools for its citizens. They were segregated schools, and none were established for Indians. The ten years from 1875 to 1885 can aptly be called the "Decade of Despair" for the Indians of Robeson County. Not only were they denied schools of their own, but they were now made brutally aware of their lack of recognition as a people. They were unacceptable to the white community, and resisted being fitted into the mold of segregation which was then being shaped for the Negro. The Robeson Indians responded with determination to improve their situation. They set as their goals the development of educational facilities for their children. Their goals in education were to become a basis for pride and dignity, as well as providing recognition of the people as an identifiable race with deep roots as original owners of the land, as well as part of the beginnings of the nation.

The Indians, fortunately, had an advocate of their cause in the North Carolina General Assembly in the person of the Honorable Hamilton McMillan of Red Springs, representative from Robeson County. As noted in Chapter One, McMillan investigated the origins of the Robeson Indians and concluded that they were descendants of the "Lost Colony" and a tribe of coastal Indians he mislabeled the "Croatans." Consequently, he sponsored and successfully supported legislation giving the Indians of Robeson County a legal designation and the privilege of having their own public schools, under their own direction. The two significant provisions of the law were: Section 1. "That the said Indians and their descendants shall hereafter be designated and known as the Croatan Indians;" and Section 2. "That said Indians and their descendants shall have separate schools for their children, school committees of their own race and color and shall be allowed to select teachers of their own choice. . ."

There is no evidence, however, that any public schools were immediately established for their benefit. This was due in part to the limited funds provided for that purpose, but primarily to the lack of qualified teachers. Because there had been no schools open to Indians since 1835, the illiteracy rate was extremely high. There were a few people who possessed sufficient education to teach others. Leaders of the Indian community knew that what they really needed, in order to make progress in education, was a centralized institution offering studies from the elementary to the normal (teacher-training) level. At the urging of the Indians, Hamilton McMillan sponsored, and the legislature passed "An Act to establish a normal school in the county of Robeson."[1]

This initial act created a corporation under the control of seven trustees, charged with the responsibility of "maintaining a school of high grade for teachers of the Croatan race in North Carolina." The law specified that "all those who shall enjoy the privileges of said school as students shall previously obligate themselves to teach the youth of the Croatan race for a stated period." Finally, the legislature appropriated five hundred dollars for the "payment of services rendered for teaching and for other purposes." The responsibility for obtaining a suitable structure and for acquiring other needed facilities was left to the trustees. The first Board of Trustees was composed of The Reverend W. L. Moore, Preston Locklear, James Oxendine, James Dial, Sr., J. J. Oxendine, Isaac Brayboy, and Olin Oxendine. All of these men worked diligently to turn this legislation into reality. The end product was the Croatan Normal School.

Since neither the state nor the federal government had ever before assumed any responsibility for their welfare, most of the Indians were wary about the legislation establishing the Normal School. The majority shared suspicions borne of fifty years of discrimination. It was difficult for them to believe that the whites would do something for their advancement. As a result, when W. L. Moore called a meeting to implement the provisions of this law, very few attended. Only with great difficulty could Moore arouse interest in the project and raise funds for land acquisition and construction of a building. Even then, he found it necessary to contribute $200 of his own funds and to devote his energies full time to the school, so that it could open.

The first college building, a two-story structure, was located on a one-acre site purchased for $8. The original building would have cost about $1,000, had not the people given so much of the material and labor. The Croatan Normal School opened its doors in the fall of 1887 with an enrollment of fifteen students, the first state-supported school of any type for the Robeson Indians. From this extremely modest beginning, Pembroke State University has emerged. Since W. L. Moore had completed four years of normal

---

1. See Appendix B for pertinent legislation concerning the problems of education and identity among the Lumbee Indians.

The first building of the Indian Normal School. This building was constructed by the Indian people in 1887, with an enrollment of fifteen. It served as their principal educational facility until the school was moved to its present site in 1909.
—*Photo courtesy of Elmer Hunt*

Frank H. Epps, Lumbee educator who served the people for more than thirty years. He is well remembered as principal of Magnolia High School in Robeson County, North Carolina.

school prior to moving to Robeson County, and had played a major role in founding the school, it was only natural that he was elected to be the first principal and teacher, a position he filled for the next three years.

The first years of the Croatan Normal School are a record of continued struggle and frustration. Although the 1889 state legislature increased the school's annual appropriation to $1,000, a sum it would continue to receive for many years afterwards, the school was still inadequately funded in order to erase the educational deficiencies of the Indian community, a condition caused by many years of neglect. In 1890, Moore wrote to the Office of Indian Affairs in Washington, seeking financial assistance, saying, "The people for which I am officially interested have as a general thing grown up without so much as the rudiments of education, yet the youth who have had (to some degree) better opportunites for educating themselves show that the moral, intellectual, and social aptitudes in them are real. Can not something be obtained to assist them in a normal school for them?" The answer Moore received was disheartening. T. J. Morgan, Commissioner of Indian Affairs, replied, "While I regret exceedingly that the provisions made by the State of North Carolina seem to be entirely inadequate, I find it quite impracticable to render any assistance at this time. The Government is responsible for the education of something like 36,000 Indian children and has provisions for less than half this number. So long as the immediate wards of the Government are so insufficiently provided for, I do not see how I can consistently render any assistance to the Croatans or any other civilized tribes." A shortage of money continued to be a critical problem for the Croatan School for many years to come.

During its early history, the school, reflecting existing conditions, offered mainly elementary-level work, although some normal classes were provided. In 1905, Mr. D. F. Lowry received the first diploma issued by the Croatan Normal School, for completing its "Scientific Course." He was the first graduate of the Indian school. Early in 1974, the Reverend D. F. Lowry, now 94 years of age and still active, recalled his student days and noted that the class work offered in those first years of the school had not been standardized. Students were allowed to study "anything they could handle."

In 1909, the decision was made to move the school nearer to Pembroke, center of the Lumbee Indian community. Land was purchased at the site now occupied by the university. With $3,000 appropriated by the legislature, a new building was constructed. From this point on, the institution slowly but steadily improved, both in quality of instruction and in number of students.

In 1911, because the name "Croatan" had become a label of derision, the General Assembly changed the name of the people to "Indians of Robeson County," and the name of the school to "Indian Normal School of Robeson County," a change that pleased nobody and settled nothing. The Indians wanted a more clearly identifiable name for themselves, and in 1913 the legislature re-named them the "Cherokee Indians of Robeson County." The school became the "Cherokee Indian Normal School of Robeson County," a name it would bear for the next twenty-eight years. Moreover, the legislature enacted a law transferring, by deed, the property of the Indian Normal School to the State Board of Education. This agency was also given the authority to appoint the Board of Trustees.

The first surge of progress for the college came during the superintendency of Prof. T. C. Henderson (1918-1922). As a result of Henderson's energetic policies, the faculty was increased, new high school courses were offered, vocational courses were introduced, and a summer school was begun. Also, in 1921, due to the efforts of Judge L. R. Varser of Lumberton, member of the state legislature, the state appropriated $75,000 for a new and more modern building. This structure, completed in 1923, became "Old Main," the oldest building on the campus of Pembroke State University, a controversial structure partially destroyed by fire in 1973.

The progressive policies of Henderson were carried on by two noteworthy successors: Prof. A. B. Riley (1922-1926), and Prof. S. B. Smithy (1926-1929). Under Mr. Riley, construction of needed facilities was carried forward, the summer school enlarged, and, in 1924, the high school was accredited by the State Board of

Education. The decision was also made to phase out the elementary grades still being taught at the school by 1928. In 1925, legislation was enacted placing the Board of Trustees under the control of the governor, where it remains to this day. Finally, in August, 1926, the Board of Trustees determined that the school should begin to fulfill the purpose for which it had been established—teacher preparation and training. A regular two-year normal course was added to the curriculum. Professor Smithy, who came from the faculty of the University of North Carolina at Chapel Hill, inaugurated the first full-fledged normal class at the Pembroke institution in the fall of 1926. With steady improvement in normal work, the school graduated its first class of ten members on June 1, 1928, and Prof. Smithy was able to announce at the commencement exercises that the institution had been accredited by the State as a "Standard Normal School." By the fall of 1928 the school was offering only secondary and normal school courses.

Throughout the early history of the institution, few men served it more faithfully or had a more profound impact on it than the Reverend Oscar R. Sampson. He was associated with the school as a student, teacher, and trustee for more than thirty years. His greatest contributions were unquestionably his recognition of the value of education as a means to advancement, and the encouragement he gave his people to take advantage of the opportunities offered by the school. The death of Mr. Sampson in 1928 deprived the school and the community of a positive guiding influence.

The coming of the "Great Depression" in 1929 definitely had an adverse effect on the progress of the Pembroke institution, but adversity was nothing new. Under superintendents J. E. Sawyer (1929-1935) and G. C. Maughon (1935-1940) the school, frequently operating with reduced funds, nevertheless continued to take steps that augured well for the future. During this decade of economic crisis, a college curriculum was gradually added, and at the spring commencement of 1940, the first four-year college degrees were awarded to five members of the graduating class. In 1936 the college added its first full-time librarian. Also, it began a program of instruction for deaf students, but this program was unfortunately discontinued in 1939 because of its expense and the difficulty of securing trained teachers. The high school, long an integral part of the institution, was moved to a new, off-campus site in 1939. In recognition of the fact that the school was truly an institution of higher learning, the 1941 state legislature officially changed the name of the school to Pembroke State College for Indians, later shortened to Pembroke State College.

In 1942, the board of trustees selected Dr. Ralph Wellons as president of the college. The choice was an excellent one. Dr. Wellons brought to the position a strong academic background. At least three major developments marked his administration. First, like all institutions of higher learning, Pembroke State had to cope with an influx of students following the end of World War II. Indian veterans returned home more aware than ever of the need for education and many took advantage of the G.I. Bill to gain a college degree. For those students who desired a skill, the college operated a trade school for a period of several years. Second, the need for an enlarged physical plant became obvious. The result was the addition of a new administration-library building, two classroom buildings, a president's house, and plans for future expansion. And third, it was during Dr. Wellons' administration that the college was opened to all races on an equal basis.

From the founding of the institution to the year 1945, enrollment was limited to Indians of Robeson County. In 1945, the privilege of admission was extended to include persons from any Indian group recognized by the federal government. From 1940 to 1953 Pembroke was the only state-supported, four-year college for Indians in the nation. Then, in 1953, the legislature amended the statutes giving the trustees of the college the authority to admit "any other persons of the Indian or white races" who may be approved by that governing board. In May, 1953, the board approved admission of whites up to a maximum of forty percent of the total enrollment. The United States Supreme Court decision outlawing segregation in 1954 prompted the board to remove all racial restrictions. Pembroke State was one of the first southern colleges to take this step. Today, it serves all races equally in the

Top. The Reverend W. L. Moore (1857-1930), founder and first headmaster of Croatan Normal School.

—Photo courtesy of the family

Center. The Board of Trustees for the Indian Normal School, 1935-1936. An all-Indian Board of Trustees for an all-Indian educational institution.

—Photo from Indian Normal School Catalog

Oscar R. Sampson. A pioneer in Lumbee education who served on the Pembroke State University Board of Trustees for thirty years.

—Photo courtesy of Lucy Sampson

effort to understand and to cope with modern society and its demands.

In 1956, Dr. Wellons retired. As his successor, the board of trustees chose Dr. Walter J. Gale (1956-1962). The six years that Dr. Gale directed the affairs of the college were primarily years of consolidation, strengthening of the academic program, and preparation for future growth. In September, 1962, Dr. Gale resigned to work in the student aid division of the Department of Health, Education, and Welfare in Washington, D.C. He was replaced by Dr. English E. Jones, the first Lumbee to head the institution since W. L. Moore, the first to serve as president of the college, and the first to serve as chancellor of the school since it was made a campus of the Consolidated University of North Carolina. This latter change was brought about in 1971, when the state's system of higher education was reorganized.

Paralleling the development of a four-year institution of higher education was the evolution of a system of elementary and secondary schools to serve the Lumbee people. In the 1920's, as the college performed its primary function of training teachers, and phased out its non-college level programs, a network of schools began to grow up which ultimately made the Lumbees, taken as a group, the best-educated Indians in America. In fact, by the 1930's there were six all-Indian high schools and more than a dozen elementary feeder schools operating in Robeson County. Most of the Indian high school graduates who chose to attend college, enrolled at Pembroke State. The few who went away did so because they believed they could receive a more specialized education out of the area.

While the Lumbees have been proud of their educational achievements as a people, they have long known that these achievements came at great cost and at a slower pace than was necessary. This was particularly true concerning the matter of public schools. During the 1920's, the question of Indian schools was of overriding importance partly because of the tri-racial nature of Robeson County and partly because of the existence of a group known as the "Smilings."

Although the origin of the "Smilings" is uncertain, they appear to have been the product of miscegenation and to have migrated to Robeson County from the area of Sumter, South Carolina, after World War I. While the Lumbees sympathized with the plight and problems of this group, they were unwilling to allow them into the schools they had fought so hard and suffered so grievously to get. In 1921, because of Lumbee determination to preserve their schools, the General Assembly of North Carolina passed "An Act for the Protection of the Indian Public Schools of Robeson County." The act, which established a powerful committee composed totally of Indians, provided that: ". . . all questions affecting the race of those applying for admission to public schools of Robeson County for the Indian race only, and all such questions coming from the County Board of Education, or any school board in the county shall be forthwith removed before said (Indian) committee for hearing." The law further stated that in case of a vacancy, the remaining committee members were to appoint an Indian to fill the position. The group was commonly referred to as the "Committee of Five" and was originally comprised of Ralph Lowery, James B. Oxendine, J. E. Woodell, W. M. Wilkins, and Calvin Locklear.

The law assuring the Lumbees control over admission policies in their schools was amended in 1929. The size of the committee was increased to seven, and the normal school was made subject to its power. This committee technically existed until 1954, when the United States Supreme Court issued its desegregation order. The "Smilings" were eventually provided a one-teacher elementary school, but their educational needs were not fully met until 1957, when they were admitted to schools of their choice. For this group's lack of educational opportunity, the Robeson County Board of Education, the whites, and the Indians must all share resonsibility. Only the Blacks are blameless in this matter.

The power to determine who was eligible to attend their schools did not, however, mean that the Lumbees controlled finances, the appointment of teachers, or many other facets of the local educational system that directly affected them. A review of the minutes of the county board of education reveals many of the petty frustrations and absurdities with which the Lumbees had to

Lumbees and their horses. In recent years horseback riding has returned as a favorite pastime.
—*Photo by William P. Revels*

Prospect High School basketball team and cheerleaders, 1973-1974. Lumbee Indians compose both the basketball team and the cheerleading squad. Out of a total of 978 students, less than one percent are non-Indian.
—*Photo by William P. Revels*

cope. For much of the twentieth century the board was all white and it generally dealt with the Indians in a patronizing fashion. As only one example, when a vacancy occurred on a local school committee, the Indians were generally expected to appear before the board, usually accompanied by a white lawyer, in order to get an Indian, equally as qualified as the former incumbent, appointed to the position.[2] It would appear that the board played this game to remind the Indians that it had control over their schools, and that they were second-class citizens in terms of the power structure. In 1942, a Lumbee was hired by a local committee to teach at the school they supervised, but the county board refused to approve him. Despite the board's negative action, the man taught in the local school for the entire year, receiving no compensation. He was an excellent teacher, a respected gentleman, and a church leader in his community, but he was also an Indian Republican in a solidly Democratic area. That was enough to disqualify him for the teaching post he sought. Sometimes the Indians obtained facilities because it was advantageous for certain whites. For example, a school was approved for the children of an Indian community when its delegation was accompanied by a white politician who went before the board and pointed out that ". . . the lack of the convenience of a community school in that area is working a hardship on the landowners in that they cannot secure the better Indian tenants because of the lack of school facilities." While this speaks well for the Indian parents who wanted education for their children, it is a bitter condemnation of the system that controlled their lives.

In the 1970's the Lumbees moved vigorously to acquire a greater voice in the administration of the county schools, an issue of special concern because at the time sixty percent of the students in the system were Indian. Of the eleven-member county school board, there were four Indian members, two black, and five white. A related issue of concern to the Lumbees has been the "double-voting" system. Under this system, the townspeople, their own schools controlled by city boards of education, also vote for

2. Local committees were appointed by the County Board of Education which was all white. Local committeemen directed the affairs of the community schools under the supervision of the County Board of Education.

101

county board members, frequently determining the winners. As a result of this situation, the composition of the board has generally been such that the county people, and especially the Indians, found it to be unrepresentative and unresponsive to their needs and wishes. The legality of this system has been questioned. Adequate representation on policy-making boards is essential to the development of programs designed to meet the needs of the people. It should be stated, however, that the Lumbees have always sought justice, not necessarily "all-Indian" schools. The teaching of Indian history, culture, and heritage in the public school curriculum, as a rich addition to the learning process, has always been the Lumbees' goal. They have worked to create first-rate public schools of high quality, providing a curriculum of practical usefulness in a complex world. But educational changes in Robeson county, just as is the case elsewhere, have been achieved only with immense effort and patience.

Pembroke State University is the apex of the area's educational system. Now open to all races, considerable pride is taken in its growth and progress, and the multi-racial composition of its student body has been accepted. At the same time, the "de-Indianization" of a university founded by Indians was distressing. The Indian people have strongly supported the concept that the university ought not to forget its past, nor its special relationship to the Lumbee people. It should serve the state without ceasing to be a part of the Indian community.

Much of the growth of Pembroke State University can be attributed to the efforts of Chancellor English Jones. During his tenure as a chief executive officer, the school has been transformed from a small, relatively unknown college to a progressive, regional university. The physical plant has been enlarged. The student population has grown, and the quality of the academic program has been improved. The university is a cornerstone of Indian achievement and exemplifies the ability of the Lumbees to move with the times, involving all of the people in the success of this unique educational institution. It is a matter of pride that the following accomplishments can be credited to the leadership of Dr. Jones, Lumbee Chancellor: Thirteen new academic or service structures have been built, including a science building, business administration building, library, six-story women's dormitory, and a physical education complex. Construction of a $1,800,000 auditorium has been assured and a $1,300,000 classroom building funded for this biennium. The restoration and renovation of the oldest building on campus, officially known as "Memorial Auditorium" but affectionately called *Old Main* has been assured. In 1974, the total value of university facilities and land was $15,000,000. The campus occupies 63 acres located along the western edge of the town of Pembroke. Student enrollment was approximately 1,950 in the 1973-74 academic year. The university's summer school serves an estimated 2,100 students during two five-week sessions. Each year the new students who begin their studies at Pembroke State University come better prepared to do college-level work. The university's Human Services Center involves faculty, students, and townspeople in a broad program of community involvement.

The Lumbee Indians, together with the public and academic community, have noted that rapid growth could weaken a school academically by diluting the quality of instruction, but this has not happened at Pembroke State. To the contrary, the quality of the academic program has improved steadily over the last decade. In 1974, of 115 faculty members, approximately 45 percent held doctorates; the rest had at least masters' degrees, with the exception of two who held equivalencies. All faculty members were brought down to a teaching load of twelve semester hours in 1974, giving the individual teacher more time for preparation, for his professional activities, and for attention to his personal students. New, more relevant programs, such as minority studies with an emphasis on Indian history and culture, were introduced.

The university established a Continuing Education Division, designed to offer educational opportunities to mature members of the community who are unable to meet the demands of a regular academic year program. Under this division, individuals within commuting distance can complete their first year of college study by enrolling in evening classes on the Pembroke State University campus. Also under consideration in 1974 was a graduate program.

Pembroke State College becomes a University.
—Photo by Elmer Hunt

The university serves a thirteen-county area in the state. It is a fully accredited member of the Southern Association of Colleges and Universities in good standing. In 1969 this accreditation was extended for an additional ten years. The university has also been accredited by the National Council for the Accreditation of Teacher Education. This means that the teacher-preparation program meets national standards. Certainly the founders of this educational institution would be proud of its achievements. A high point of Pembroke State's recent history was the gaining of university status in 1969. To achieve this goal, the entire college community, students, faculty and administration, joined hands and worked together for the common good. The college was supported by its board of trustees, by the citizens of the area, and by local representatives in both Houses of the General Assembly. University status meant added prestige, a broadening and enlargement of the academic program, and a chance to gain better financial assistance from the federal government and from private sources. It also meant new responsibilities and opportunities to prepare the students for their chosen professions.

One of the least appreciated aspects of the university is its economic contribution to the region it serves. The students who attend Pembroke State bring thousands of dollars into the area. The university itself employed 224 people in 1974, including faculty, with an average monthly payroll of $160,000. For the 1973-75 biennium, the capital improvements budget was $2 million, at least some of which remains in the county as wages, or spent for local services and materials. Pembroke State University had an asset of approximately $18 million to Robeson and surrounding counties during 1974, including the physical plant, the land, and all budgets for maintenance and operation.

Despite the obstacles they have had to overcome, the Lumbee Indians have enjoyed remarkable success in acquiring educational facilities and in using these facilities to change and improve their situation. There have always been problems, and doubtless there will always be problems. But rarely has the promise of education been more clearly perceived by a people, nor more advantageously used. Those Lumbee forefathers who founded what is now Pembroke State University have good reason for pride in "what their hands hath wrought."

LUMBEE RELIGIONS

Throughout their recorded history, the Lumbee Indians have practiced the white man's religions. Just when Native American religion lost its influence is unknown. One may assume that the process began in the late sixteenth century, when the settlers of the John White colony merged with the Hatteras Tribe at Croatan. When the Scots moved into the area of Robeson County in the early eighteenth century, the Lumbees were already Christians, though they had no formal religious organizations until the next century. Having no formal churches in those early days, they worshipped in private homes, under the shade of bush arbors or, for part of the nineteenth century, infrequently in churches of the white people.

The missionaries who worked long and hard in earlier times to convert the American Indian did not come to Robeson County in any great numbers. If the Indian author Vine Deloria is correct in his assessment of the role of missionaries in Native American history, then the Lumbees were probably fortunate. In his book, *Custer Died for Your Sins,* Deloria states, "One of the major problems of the Indian people is the missionary. It has been said of missionaries that when they arrived they had only one Book and we had the land; now we have the Book and they have the land. An old Indian once told me that when the missionaries arrived they fell on their knees and prayed. Then they got up, fell on the Indians and preyed." The general lack of missionaries in Lumbee country is noteworthy, because it signifies that the people were already practicing a form of Christianity and were, in the eyes of the white man, "more civilized" than most other Native Americans.

It is uncertain when the first churches were built to serve the Lumbee community, but whenever it was, it is certain that they were primarily affiliated with the Baptist and Methodist sects. According to tradition, some of the first church buildings among the Lumbees were those named New Hope, Thessalonica, Union

Chapel, Old Dogwood, Reedy Branch, Burnt Swamp, Old Prospect, New Jerusalem, and Saint Annah.[3]

The first formal religious organization was begun by the Lumbee Baptists in 1880, to advance the ideals and achieve the goals of Christianity. A group of Indian Baptists met at the Burnt Swamp Church, with Cary Wilkins, a Lumbee, serving as moderator, and organized the "Burnt Swamp Association of the Mixed Race," which has continued to serve the people and grown with steady progress. A few years later the name of the organization was changed to the "Burnt Swamp Association of the Croatan Race," a result of the legislation adopted by the North Carolina General Assembly in 1885, which designated the Indians of Robeson County as Croatans. Just as the association had dropped the label "Mixed Race," so did they later drop the name "Croatan."

In 1973, the Ninety-Sixth Annual Session of the Burnt Swamp Association of North Carolina reported a membership of more than six thousand members in forty-two churches. The membership of the associated churches is almost one hundred percent Indian, with the notable exception of Berea Baptist Church, located near the Pembroke State University Campus. Although a number of the churches in the Burnt Swamp Association were served by part-time ministers at the time of this writing, there were also several full-time Lumbee ministers and one full-time white minister, Jimmy Fox, who has been described as a "Lumbee in all but name." His primary service has been to fight for the rights of all human beings and to insist that his congregation actually practice the teachings of Christianity. Although he was not the first pastor serving the Lumbee community to admit a Black to his congregation, he has been the most insistent that Blacks are welcome to join the Christian fellowship. While this stand almost caused the church, in the words of one member, "to explode," the tensions have been resolved and Rev. Fox's church functions effectively as a tri-racial organization. Although the Burnt Swamp Association found it necessary in earlier times to follow a rule stating that no two associated churches would be established within five miles of

---

3. The name Saint Annah is curiously an early English spelling for Saint Anne; how the Lumbee church acquired this name is not known but it might be one more bit of evidence to support the "Lost Colony" theory.

each other unless the churches were divided by a stream, it had three churches with memberships in excess of 350 each in 1974 and no longer has it had to worry about interassociation competition. Indeed, the renovated Harper's Ferry Church, with a modern plant worth approximately $400,000, fittingly located on the banks of the Lumbee River, stands as a monument to the strength and growth of the Burnt Swamp Association.

The second largest denomination among the Lumbees is the Methodist Church. The Methodists are split into two groups, the North Carolina Conference of the United Methodist Church and the Holiness Methodist Church of the Lumbee River Annual Conference. The latter is commonly known as the Lumbee Methodist Conference. Though the division occurred in 1900, the roots of the factionalism go back into the nineteenth century. The leaders of Lumbee Methodism at the time of the split were Rev. Henry H. Lowry and Rev. William Luther Moore. Lowry led the segment that broke away from the existing Methodist organization, whereas Moore remained as the leader of the established conference. It would be easy to blame the division on personality differences or rivalry for leadership; however, this does not appear to be the case. Lowry and Moore remained life-long friends until Moore's death in 1931. The reason for the formation of the Lumbee Methodist Conferences was to bring self-determination to the Lumbee people, to create an organization in which the Lumbees made the decisions from top to bottom. At their organizational meeting of October 26, 1900, they stated that their purpose was to organize a "Conference for the Indian descent."

Because Henry H. Lowry led a group of Lumbees out of the Methodist Church in order to form an all-Indian conference, the established Methodist Episcopal Church, at its Quarter Conference meeting of September 20, 1902, passed a resolution expelling Lowry and his followers. The resolution stated that "H. H. Lowry, Israel Locklear, Mahoney Locklear, C. C. Lowry and those members who have joined them are not members of the Methodist Episcopal Church." The Quarterly Conference went on to warn the ministers of the new conference, that they had no right to perform marriage ceremonies nor to baptize converts.

Reverend Henry H. Lowry became the first Presbyter of the Lumbee Conference in 1900, and served in that capacity until his death in 1935. He was succeeded by his nephew, J. R. Lowry, who served as Presbyter until 1937, and then was elevated to the position of Bishop, an office he filled for the next twenty-two years. A few months before the death of J. R. Lowry, his brother, M. L. Lowry, was chosen to fill the post of Bishop and served until incapacitated in 1962, thus ending the Lowry dynasty of sixty-two years in Lumbee Methodism. Since 1962, the Lumbee Conference has been led by Bishops Belton Bullard (1962-68), J. W. Locklear (1968-73), and Ward Clark (1973-present).

In addition to his ministerial duties, Henry H. Lowry fathered nine children and, in the face of adverse conditions, saw that each acquired an education with which he or she could serve others. This family gave the Lumbees their second and fourth medical doctors, their first pharmacist, their first minister with a divinity degree, and their first registered nurse. Moreover, the four other children all became educators in the Lumbee community. One son, Elmer T. Lowry, was an extremely successful principal of Pembroke High School for many years.

There were more than sixteen hundred members worshipping in the seven churches of the Lumbee Conference in 1974. Their church buildings are as modern as any in the rural area of Robeson County. Until recently, the Lumbee Methodists had no minimum salary for their ministers, nor did they require their member churches to contribute any specific sum of money for the continuance of the Conference, a situation that produced a certain amount of financial instability. Yet, as one Lumbee Methodist put it, "Love many, trust few, always paddle your own canoe."

W. L. Moore, the other pioneer of Indian Methodism, saw no particular advantage to an all-Indian Conference and so remained with the Methodist Episcopal Church. Today, the foundation he laid supports the North Carolina Conference of the United Methodist Church, which has a Lumbee membership of eighteen hundred. There are ten churches in the "White Conference," so-called because of its affiliation with national Methodism. One of the churches in the conference, Prospect United Methodist, is believed to have the largest membership of any Indian church in North America. With an enrollment of more than six hundred, the church is located in the heart of the Lumbee population. Among the membership there are no Blacks and only one white, a man who married a Lumbee girl and now considers himself a part of the Indian community. The Prospect Church budget for 1974 was $53,000. It possesses a physical plant worth $500,000, but more important, this church is the center of the Prospect community and had an impact on that community seldom matched in any rural area in the United States.

That W. L. Moore is one of the most important figures in Lumbee history is indisputable. This remarkable man was both a preacher and missionary, founding churches throughout Robeson County. He was a man who always tried to help the poor, of which there were a great many in the late nineteenth and early twentieth centuries. His contributions were not limited to religious work; he was also an outstanding educator and the patriarch of a family that produced many successful businessmen, craftsmen, educators, and leaders. Perhaps the respect the community has for Moore is best revealed in the comments of a hundred-year-old Lumbee who said; "He was the best we ever had. Don't have no ministers today, not like he was. People had confidence in him. He was a good Christian."

Among other churches serving the Lumbee community is the Church of Jesus Christ of Latter Day Saints. The Mormons came to Pembroke in the early 1960's with a number of hard workers. Stressing recreation and instruction, the Mormon buses were ready at the conclusion of the school day to pick up the children for an evening of play and training. Among their teachings the Mormons emphasized their belief that American Indians are descended from the Lost Tribes of Israel, a belief that gives Indians a special place in their religion. Out of this missionary activity came a new church in Pembroke, for which the Mormons solicited no local funds. Mormon efforts in the area resulted in several Lumbees attending Brigham Young University in Utah. One of these students recently summarized the reason for the Mormon successes when he said: "The Mormons seem to care for poor people when others

Hopewell Methodist Church, a member of the Lumbee River Holiness Methodist Conference which grew out of a split with the Methodist Episcopal Conference in 1900. There remains to this day two Methodist Conferences among the Lumbees, with each having approximately the same number of members.

—Photo by William P. Revels

111

have forgotten them."

Other denominations active in Lumbee country are the Free-will Baptists, Church of God, Pentecostal Holiness, Plymouth Brethren, Assembly of God, Independents, Jehovah's Witnesses, and Seventh Day Adventists. The latter two are few in number and generally well-integrated with the whites.

There have been no Indian Presbyterian churches. This is rather surprising because southeastern North Carolina was largely settled by Scots, and Presbyterian churches for Negroes and whites have long been numerous in the area. Apparently, Blacks were drawn to Presbyterianism as a result of the social system of the Old South. In the ante-bellum years slaves were allowed to attend the church of their master, though segregated in galleries built for that purpose. Since many of the local slavemasters were Presbyterian, it was only natural that their chattels became members of that denomination. Then, when the issue of slavery split many churches into northern and southern branches, including the Presbyterian, and the Civil War brought freedom to the Blacks, the freedmen generally continued their allegiance to the church they knew, but usually affiliated with the northern division. Since the Indians of Robeson never became slaves, they couldn't become Presbyterians by that route. Furthermore, it appears there was little or no missionary spirit among the area Presbyterians in the past.

In the mid-1960's the Society of Friends came to Robeson County. The Quakers were interested in promoting community involvement, not in establishing a congregation. Their announced purpose was to seek social justice for all people. They worked to increase the registration of minority voters and to provide those new registrants with knowledge about the rudiments of the political process. Although hindsight shows the Friends to have been a moderate and positive force, they created considerable consternation among the "white establishment" at the time. Most people have recognized that Robeson County is a better place in which to live because the Quakers pushed minority involvement in the political system, thereby helping to create more representative local government.

It was also in the 1960's that the Robeson County Church and Community Center was organized, thanks largely to the efforts and support of the United Methodist Church. Reverend Robert Mangum, a Methodist minister and a powerful influence among the minorities in the area, served as the director of the Center from the beginning. Mangum consistently challenged the Christian community to come forward and deal with the basic issues confronting human beings. Although the Church and Community Center has been open to all denominations, many chose not to participate in its projects because the Center has often been involved with unpopular causes and issues. Quite simply, the Center recognized that social change cannot come without some pain, and so, guided by its philosophy of love, integrity, and holism, it dedicated itself to doing whatever it could to improve life for all Robesonians.

In addition to their support of the Church and Community Center, the United Methodist Church also attempted, through its Commission on Race and Religion, to get Blacks and Indians involved in the process of government and to help them cope with the problems they face. The Commission funded a variety of projects with a grant of $87,500. As one proud Methodist lay leader put it, "Now you see Christianity in action."

The Lumbee community, over the years, has consistently been a Christian community. Paradoxically, the devotion of the people to religion has had both good and bad consequences. On the one hand, it has been a positive force from the standpoint of moral integrity. But it has also been a negative influence in the sense that it has made some people too wary of challenging the system. An example, repeated many times in Lumbee history, involves the tenant-landlord relationship. Under this relationship, tenants experienced lives of exploitation and poverty. In part this was due to their lack of knowledge about records and receipts. It was also due to the precepts of their religion, which taught them to trust their fellowman and to believe in the immortality to come. That they might enjoy material prosperity while on earth and still make it to heaven is a realization that seems to have eluded many of the Lumbee people.

An example of a Lumbee who was both sustained and impoverished by his religion was the Reverend Z. R. Chavis, a man who

Groundbreaking ceremony for First Baptist Church of Pembroke. A group of Lumbee Indians watch their pastor break ground for their new church building.

—Photo by Elmer Hunt

Prospect Methodist Church, with a membership of six hundred, believed to be the largest Indian church in North America. Not shown, is a large, modern education building and fellowship hall. Less than one percent non-Indians live within a five-mile radius of this rural church located in the heart of Lumbee territory.

—Photo by William P. Revels

Harper's Ferry Baptist Church, member of the Burnt Swamp Baptist Association, located by the Lumbee River. The swamp in background shows big cypress, oak, and gum trees, affording homes for a variety of wildlife.

—Photo by William P. Revels

lived to be ninety-nine years old and who, though he never completed the third grade, was viewed as a great spiritual leader. In his entire life Mr. Chavis never owned a horse and buggy nor an automobile. He journeyed by foot. As an itinerant preacher, he walked considerable distances to deliver his sermons, the farthest being a monthly trip of forty miles to Fayetteville, North Carolina, which he made for a period of ten years. Reverend Chavis was so devout that he never acquired many worldly possessions. His son Jim, at the age of eighty years, remarked, "In my young days I was prejudiced against religion because of my father's tough times. I never could understand why he couldn't afford a horse and buggy. Father worked hard and kept his mind on the Lord at all times; he thought of the Lord so much that he could not do a job that required much concentration." Thus, he was never very successful as a farmer or railroader. Although Rev. Chavis died poor, he always appeared to be happy, and as he frequently said and obviously believed, "I am rich with the Lord." Unfortunately, his concern with life after death made him fatalistic concerning life on earth, and it was this attitude, shared by many Indians in the past, that helped to hinder progress and advancement in the Lumbee community.

One of the most complete sources of information concerning the Lumbees and religion exists in the *Minutes* of the Burnt Swamp Baptist Association. These records show clearly the kinds of problems and concerns the people had in the late nineteenth and early twentieth centuries, many of which have continued to the present. For example, there was genuine concern over abuses associated with alcohol, as evidenced by the establishment of a committee on temperance. In a report issued in 1881, this committee observed:

> Intemperance, or the improper use of intoxicating liquor is an evil, the qualities of which we see plainly demonstrated in every day life. The improper use of intoxicating liquors bring men of character to the polluted valley of sin and degradation, steals their money, takes away their character, robs their family of clothing and food and renders them more uncomfortable than any other evil in which they could participate. It is the

ground and the pillar upon which all evil is based directly or indirectly. All the crimes committed that deserve punishment at our common courts or in the church are traceable to whiskey.

The Committee concluded its report urging the association to work for an end to the sale of alcoholic beverages.

Another great concern of the churches at the turn of the century was the nature of the literature being disseminated. According to the Burnt Swamp Association, the late nineteenth century was a time when people "delight in reading matter. . . of trifling merit." The same comment has often been made today.

While many historians consider that a concern with temperance and the nature of literature are indications of a provincial mind, viewed in perspective these churchmen were simply interested in the moral uplifting of their people. While the correctness of their approach might be challenged, their motives are unimpeachable. Indeed, their interest in the salvation of their people was so deep that they placed considerable emphasis both on "domestic missions" and "sabbath schools." They looked upon missions as "the very genius of Christianity. . . To convert the whole world to Christianity is the desire of every good Christian." And they felt this work should begin at home. In fact, the "sabbath schools" were to be a primary agency for the conversion of local people. The purpose of these schools was ". . . to soften the hearts of the recipients for the reception of the gospel."

The greatest emphasis of the early churches was on education, both as an instrument of progress and a standard of morality. According to the Burnt Swamp Association *Minutes,*

Education implies a knowledge of books and how to reduce their contents to practice. . . Viewing the subject of general education through all the avocations of life we notice it terminates with success. Education is needed at the bar, in the cornfield, in the domestic business of the household, in conducting the affairs of government, in carrying on the cause of Christ, and in fact it is needed in every business avocation of life.

116

The Association expressed the feeling of much of the Lumbee community when it said "education. . . is the only way our race can be brought from the valley of ignorance to the summit of intelligence."

For the modern urban dweller, self-satisfied with his own "sophistication," it is very difficult to appreciate the importance and value of religion to rural people, many of whom live their lives in relative isolation and within narrow geographical boundaries. Although religion is important as a guiding philosophy, it serves many purposes besides the moralistic-salvationist one. Religion in a rural area is an extremely important social force. It brings people together for the exchange of ideas and information, and it provides opportunity for a host of other social functions, such as picnics, circle meetings, and charitable activities. The church has been the focal point of community spirit. It can and often does instruct its members about political matters. It has worked for progressive change, and preserved the best of the past. While the Lumbees have enjoyed these benefits from their religion, they enjoy other benefits as excellent farmers and outdoorsmen. Their daily contact with nature makes their religion an integral part of their existence. In short, Lumbee religion and life are intertwined in such a fashion as to give the people the opportunity for joy in this world while preparing for the next. Thus, the Lumbees have established their relationship with God and their religion through the centuries, in much the same spirit of adoration as their Indian ancestors had. The difference is only in the type and structure of worship.

CONCLUSIONS

Education and religion have been vital forces in the history of the Lumbee Indians. Faith has sustained them in their struggle against adversity, while education has been the instrument that helped them overcome repression and moved them forward, as they sought successfully to improve the quality of their lives. Considering the limited opportunities and advantages available to them, few people have accomplished more on their own than have the Lumbee Indians of North Carolina. Unquestionably, education and religion, combined with their determination and pride, have helped lift them "out of darkness."

Mt. Olive Baptist Church, built circa 1885, is a member of the Burnt Swamp Baptist Association, organized in 1880.

—*Photo courtesy of Mrs. Fanny Locklear*

5

Old Times
Not Forgotten

Folklore is an important source of information about any people lacking written records of their past, providing insight into the beliefs, interests, humor, and lifestyle of the people. Fortunately, the Lumbees are, by their own characterization, a "talking" people, a point they often illustrate with the story of the nineteenth-century Indian who was captured by slavers, sold to a master for a life of bondage and toil, but who, with great vigor, persuaded his new master that he was a victim of circumstances and by rights a free man. Convinced that a mistake had been made, the master released the "talker," losing his considerable investment in the process. Whether the story is true or apocryphal, it illustrates both the willingness of the Lumbees to talk and their skill as talkers.

Many elderly Lumbees tell stories they heard as children, or relate tales of their own experiences. Most of the stories are about ghosts and spirits, treasure, witchcraft and conjuring, social activities, and death. While a number of the elderly story-tellers are educated and well-informed, they nevertheless believe the stories they tell to be true, based on actual happenings.

One of the most prolific Lumbee story-tellers is Early Bullard, a former judge of the Robeson County Recorders Court, an octogenarian who has remained sharp of mind. A central character in several of Bullard's stories is Aaron Carter, a man of somewhat mystical qualities. According to one story, Carter had a bitter enemy who desired to kill him but who never succeeded because he was unable to find a gun that would fire while aimed at Carter's body. Thus, Carter died a natural rather than violent death. Aaron Carter is also the subject of another oft-repeated story. People of the Prospect Community near Pembroke tell of passing Carter on the road and stopping to offer him a ride. Carter's inevitable response was, "I'll walk." When the travelers arrived at their destination, Carter was always there to greet them.

Stories of individuals with unusual powers or accomplishments are not unusual among a people who have known years of isolation, whether imposed by geography or segregation. Under such circumstances, individual achievements take on added meaning, becoming a source both of interest and pride. A tale that illustrates the point is that of the Lumbee who walked to Florida to find his daughter, located her, and then walked back to North Carolina with her. Another Lumbee legend says that Bill Brewington of Sampson County, North Carolina, once danced for the King of England. His descendants claim that he performed a smooth dance with a glass of wine on his head. The narrator of this story concluded it with the remark: "The serene dancer never broke a glass."

Another prominent individual who has acquired respected status in Lumbee folklore, for reasons of spiritual love and charitable acts rather than for skill or endurance, is the Reverend W. L. Moore, a leading Methodist minister, and one of the founders of Pembroke State University. Moore was renowned as a speaker and preferred by many people to officiate at burial services. He lent an air of dignity to any service; a human being in death was honored no matter what his station in life might have been. Yet, despite his formal education, Moore believed in spirits, and always seemed to know when he was going to be asked to preach at a funeral. Generally, some unusual sound around his house would occur, a night or two before the passing of someone in the community. One of the late Reverend Moore's daughters told of the night that there was a frightful noise in their house, a noise that sounded as if there were a hundred children running down a hall. Moore calmed his family, saying, "Have no fear, for that spirit you hear only means I am going to preach a funeral." The next day or so, someone came to report a death and asked Moore to preach at the services. Similar stories of spirits announcing death are numerous among descendants of W. L. Moore.

Unquestionably the central figure in Lumbee folklore is Henry Berry Lowrie, the epitome of individualism, a man of great strength and durability. Lowrie, as noted earlier, simply disappeared in 1872. While his mythical qualities are directly related to his ability as a fighter, the legend of the man became greater with the passage of time, partly due to frequent stories that he was still alive. While the ultimate truth may never be known, there was a natural and understandable reluctance on the part of the Lumbees to admit that Lowrie might have been a mere mortal. Consequently, as late as the 1930's, there were people who were still claiming that he occasionally came back to Robeson to attend a funeral or visit a friend and that he was living out his life in some distant state such as Florida, Oklahoma or Arizona. Of course he was always described as he looked in the period of Reconstruction, though more mature. Most of these stories fail to note that he would have been an old man by the 1930's and his appearance most certainly would have been altered by the passage of time. Still, the significance of Henry Berry Lowrie is not alone in his human accomplishments, but rather in the combination of man and myth, which is of great importance to the Lumbee community. Pride in Henry Berry rests upon his ability and courage as a fighter, as well as on his stubborn resistance to the prevailing system of injustice. Henry Berry Lowrie came to symbolize manhood to the Lumbee people. He has become their folk hero.

Belief in spirits and ghosts remained widespread as recently as several decades ago. It was common among many Lumbee families to speak of the dead, who returned to visit relatives who had not carried out requests made in an oral will. One Lumbee lady told of some household items she was to give her sister following her mother's death. The woman said: "I decided to keep the articles myself. One night my dead mother appeared before me and said, 'You have not carried out my request; take the things that

Sister is supposed to have and carry them to her tomorrow morning.' The next day the request was fulfilled and Mother never appeared again."

In earlier times apparitions seemed to enjoy appearing while the Lumbees walked in desolate places. One informant said, concerning her experience as she made her way across a stream: "The ghost would not walk ahead or behind me; it wanted to stay to my side as I crossed the stream on a slippery log. I was," she continued, "as light as a feather." A Lumbee man related how he was walking along on a bright, moonlit night, when the stillness was suddenly shattered by what sounded like a running horse. As the "animal" approached, he stepped aside to let it pass, but to his amazement, it turned and seemed to run between his legs, evoking a yell from the frightened man and a blathering response from the animal as it continued on its way down the road.

Another Lumbee used to say that he saw people without heads walking around. Frequently, when strolling with friends, he would suddenly stop and say, "I see a man with no head." He would then ask those in his presence, "Can't you see him?" Given a negative response, he would ask his companion look over his shoulder; he believed the viewer would then see the headless body that he saw. While many people believed, as no doubt some still do, in the possibility of ghosts and spirits, the stories of the use of this belief as the basis for practical jokes are legion.

Stories concerning buried treasure are another feature of Lumbee folklore. Looking for such treasure was not, however, as easy as simply digging into the earth. Old grounds where money diggers worked were spoken of as "fearful, haunted grounds"— places vaguely associated with spirits and death. For example, one informant related a story of his youth: "When I was a child, John W. Bullard (he was really known as "Bum" Bullard) sat at the tobacco barn curing tobacco and telling stories of digging for money. As the fire burned in the furnace in the late hours of the night and tobacco aroma filled the air, Bullard smoked his pipe and held our attention by telling how he went digging for money one night and had a frightening experience. Bullard said:

When you bury money you put all kinds of bones in the hole

with the money to keep prowlers away. When the money digger starts digging, all the animals of the bones buried come and stand around while you work. In order to keep the animals off you, a circle is drawn around the spot where the money is supposed to be buried. The idea is that the animals cannot cross the circle. The animals made all kinds of noise. The dogs barked, the Wildcats growled, the rattlers sang, while the men let the dirt fly. When you dig for money you don't speak. If you speak, the money moves—one foot everytime you say something. Once I dug to a pot of money; I was ready to pick it up, but when I said, "I have it," the pot disappeared.

When digging for hidden money it's also said that one must never use a shovel that was used to dig a grave; if you do and the shovel hits the container, it will disappear. While stories still abound about buried treasure, apparently no one has yet succeeded in discovering a way both to locate and acquire such riches.

Superstitions are another facet of the Lumbee past. While modern Americans deny belief in the supernatural and tend to view superstitions as popular notions, practices and sayings that cannot be proven scientifically or logically, the simple fact is, despite their disclaimers, most people are superstitious in one degree or another, at every level and stage of societal development. Superstitions are based on assumptions about causes and effects in the everyday world. They reflect the desire of people to understand and explain the experiences of their lives. Present-day Americans may claim to be free of supernatural influences but their habits of knocking on wood, or carrying lucky charms, all point to the strong hold that belief in the supernatural still has over men.

One aspect of such Lumbee beliefs was faith in the power of cup readers who continued to practice their magic on a regular basis into the 1930's. According to a number of sources, the outstanding cup reader was Nepsie Brayboy, who is credited with numerous mystical accomplishments. One Lumbee tells how he lost all his keys. Having searched for them without success, he finally went to Mrs. Brayboy who read his cup and told him, "Go back home and look on the stump by the hog pen. There you will find your keys." The man did as instructed and found them. Even more impressive is the story of Nepsie Brayboy and Marcus Dial. In 1932, Mr. Dial was ninety-six years old and physically active, though his mental condition was deteriorating. Because of his senility the family tried to keep an eye on the elderly gentleman, but one day he disappeared, causing the daughter with whom he lived to go immediately to the home of a brother to ask for help. Normally, this son could track his father's steps even amidst the footprints of many people, but unfortunately it began to rain, erasing all trace of Mr. Dial's movements. The word went out among the community members that Marcus Dial was lost. As the days passed, more and more people joined what was proving to be a futile search. On the sixth day, the family sought help from Nepsie Brayboy, who told them: "Marcus was looking for his son's house and strayed off into the woods near this house." The family thought they had searched all the woods where the sons lived, but they had overlooked a son born out of wedlock. The next day, October 11, 1932, following the cup reader's instructions, the old man's body was found near the home of his illegitimate child. Several members of the family still contend the tragedy might have been averted if Nepsie Brayboy had been consulted immediately, rather than as a last resort.

The people in the community missed Marcus Dial because of his "tall" stories. A favorite tale concerned the annual trip to the beach made in covered wagons by many Indians. Describing one particular trip, Marcus told how he stopped and walked into the woods a few yards for rest and relief. He took his watch from his pants pocket and left it hanging on a bush, not thinking about it again until he had journeyed too far down the road to return. However, the next year on the annual beach trip he made a point of stopping at the same site and always claimed that his "watch was still there ticking away and had not lost a minute.'" This fine old gentleman concluded each of his stories with the same phrase, "It's the truth if I ever told it."

Conjuring was also a part of Lumbee folklore and many people both relied on and feared conjurers. According to tradition, if one wished to become a conjurer, it was necessary to sell one's soul to the devil and forget the Lord.[1] With power gained from Satan, conjuring someone became a simple matter. Take a sprig of hair from the person to be conjured, a wasp nest, and sulfur, and put all three in a jar, which is then buried. When the victim walked over the jar, he was in the conjurer's power and could be manipulated according to his wishes, like a checker player moving his pieces in a game. Or, another way to conjure, according to a Lumbee woman, is "to put a frog in a jar, stick a needle in the frog and the person you're conjuring will hurt. If the frog dies, the conjured person will also die."

The power of authentic conjurers was believed to be great. They could perform marvelous feats, predict what was to come, and influence people merely by their presence. According to numerous sources, a "real" conjurer could be riding in a buggy, pull the horse's tail out, and then stick it back. To further show the power of conjurers, the story is told of the man who wanted to contact the spirit of his deceased wife to see how she felt about his marrying again. To establish this contact he visited a conjurer, who began to cry, saying, "I see something terrible is going to happen to you." Within the minute a bolt of lightning struck the man and killed him. Conjurers were often taken to the courthouse to sit through a trial. This was done in the hope that their presence would influence the judge and jury.

While cup readers and conjurers were important in Lumbee society, the real impact of superstition is seen in the beliefs and practices handed down from generation to generation, which affected individual actions. Most Lumbee superstitions concerned nature, love, spirits, health, death, and religion. A representative sampling of Lumbee folk beliefs is given in the following statements and stories.

If one desires for his girl friend to really fall in love with him, he should take a sprig of her hair and drop it in a fast moving stream.

A sure cure for arthritis is to have several wasps sting the

---

1. A few Lumbees distinguish between good and evil conjurers; according to these sources, good conjurers got their power from the Lord and used it to help people.

arthritic person.

If you want to learn to play a box (guitar) go to the crossroad seven times at midnight; on the seventh night the devil will meet you and teach you how to play the box.

Plant corn on the waste of the moon so it won't grow too tall.

East winds are bad for transplanting because of their drying effect. Southern winds are good for transplanting.

If the moon causes the tide of the ocean to rise and fall, can't it influence a plant.

Never wear anything new to a funeral; if you do, something bad will happen.

Someone will die when a rooster comes onto the porch and crows.

If you see a horse early in the morning wet with sweat and with his mane and tail plaited, he was ridden in the middle of the night by a witch.

A Lumbee returned home from hunting one day and sat down on his doorsteps to remove his shoes. A strange man appeared and hit him in the face with a bush. Angered, the Lumbee picked up his gun and shot the fleeing figure, confident he killed him. But when he walked over to examine the body, there was none. Inquiring among his neighbors, he learned they knew nothing of the incident. It is said that if a spirit hits you, you will die. In a few days that same Lumbee was shot and mortally wounded.

Before the days of morticians in Robeson County a girl died and was buried. For several nights afterwards the mother dreamed that her daughter had been buried alive. Believing in the power of dreams, the woman finally had the body disinterred and discovered to her horror that the girl had turned over in her casket.

Superstitious beliefs range from the frivolous to the morbid. More important, they reveal a great deal about the culture of a people. Fortunately, as Lew Barton, a Lumbee writer and historian put it, "Education and electric lights have done a lot to end much of the superstition of the people."

SOCIO-ECONOMIC ACTIVITIES

Among the Indians of Robeson and adjoining counties, school breaking was an occasion that everyone looked forward to attending. A "school breaking" signified the end of school. The people in the community made preparations for the big day far in advance. Farmers worked hard in order "to catch up" with their work so they could meet their friends at the annual event. In anticipation of the occasion, the entire family went to town to shop, traveling by foot, mule, wagon, or, for those who were more fortunate, horse and buggy. Some women bought materials from the peddler who carried his goods from house to house. The peddler generally spent the night with some of his Indian friends and was treated to a good feather bed and the finest of Indian food. His horse was fed corn and fodder, making her strong for another day's journey.

When the school-breaking day came, the crops were clean of grass and weeds and the plowing in good shape. The day began with the women preparing huge amounts of food so no one would go hungry, and with the men giving the livestock enough feed to last until "sundown." By noon, a long table was filled with good country food and it was the principal's lot to ask the blessing. As one Lumbee described it, "Sometimes the blessing was too long for a good appetite." Selling-stands for refreshments were also located on the school premises. Around the year 1900, refreshments meant lemonade for Lumbee people. Alfred Thomas usually showed up at the school-breaking with his tasty lemonade and in delight exclaimed:

> *"Lemonade made in the shade,*
> *Stirred with a spade,*
> *The best old lemonade ever made."*

As time passed, the stands added ice cream, hot dogs, and hamburgers.

Some people went home "sad" from the school-breaking day. Usually they were the ones who had brought their hard liquor, called "stumphole," which they hid in the swamp. Much of their day then consisted of making trips into the swamp to get a drink.

127

However, since the swamps were also used for restrooms, traveling to the wooded area did not necessarily mean one was drinking alcohol. The combination of festivities and liquor frequently produced some fighting and violence, with an occasional death. In almost every instance, it was a case of Indian killing Indian.

The activities were varied and included, at different times, a "Dialogue," the recitation of poetry, speeches, and musical entertainment. John R. "Whistling Rufus" Lowry played his autoharp and, as he put it, "sang and whistled at the same time." Spectators were never sure he was doing both but they always threw their small change into the hat.

When the day was over, family conversation concerned who was the best dressed girl at the affair. The women also talked of all the men who "treated" them to lemonade or food. Overeating

"Old Ben." Prior to 1900 the ox played an important part in Lumbee farming and logging operations. Here "Old Ben" and his owner Barley Locklear, pictured in 1944, stand as mute testimony to an earlier era.

—*Photo courtesy of Clifton Oxendine*

made an unhappy night for some, but the problem did not last long. Early the next morning a day's work was begun and that took care of a full stomach. After all, plowing a mule and walking thirty miles, or carrying crossties from a muddy swamp was a hard day's work and one quickly got back into his standard routine.

The practice of school-breaking lasted until the late 1950's in some Indian communities, but was finally abandoned because of its disruptive effects. Looking back on school-breaking, it was unquestionably an important social outlet. The Indian people knew little but hard work and exploitation, and this event provided a measure of relief and happiness.

For a very long time Indians in Robeson County have enjoyed hog killings as events which brought neighbors together for a day of work and fun. Pork was such an important staple in the local diet that most of the corn grown prior to World War II was fed to hogs, and most of the hogs were then butchered for home consumption. It was not unusual for an Indian family to consume from two to three thousand pounds of dressed pork in a year.

Slaughter day required a cooperative effort and neighbors who came to help brought not only their labor but knives, tables, pots, and other necessities. A big hog-killing day usually began at two o'clock in the morning. At that time roaring fires were started on which to boil pots of water. When the water was ready, it was time to knock the hogs in the head with an ax. The man wielding the ax always tried to fell the hog with one blow. Once the animal was down, it was stabbed in a major artery with a sharp knife so the blood would flow freely. The death struggle of a hog generally lasted less than five minutes. Once all the animals chosen for butchering were dead, the carcasses were taken to the yard, where they were put into a barrel of hot water, the temperature of which was approximately 150-155 degrees Fahrenheit. If a thermometer was unavailable, the hand was used to judge whether the water had reached the proper temperature. When the water was sufficiently hot, the hand could be placed in it a first and a second time, but the third time the heat would be more than the

Lumbee hog-killings. This was an annual event providing a family with enough pork for a year. Starting before daybreak, every member of the family had a job to do in the butchering process.

—Photo by William P. Revels

hand could stand and the water was judged right for the scalding process. Pine rosin was then added to the barrel of water.

When the carcass was snow white, it was ready to be gambreled, which involved cutting the outer layer of skin on the back of the rear legs and reaching some strong muscles. A stick of wood called a gambrel was put into each rear leg and three men hung the hog on a scaffold. As one Lumbee put it, "Ten or twelve hogs weighing about three hundred pounds each and waiting for the knife was a beautiful sight." A piece of corn cob about three inches long held the hog's mouth open so the blood could drain from the body.

After the hog was bled, the next step was to dress it, and some Lumbees could do this in less than a minute. The hog was first cut around the throat with the head left barely hanging on. Then the hog was ripped open, beginning between the rear legs, and all the vital organs removed. When this process was completed, it was time for the women to start their task. They scraped the intestines clean with a knife, getting them ready for sausage and pudding. Any part of the intestines not used as casings were cooked as

Lumbee farmers of the Saddletree Community. When the ox disappeared from Lumbee farms as the main work animal, he was replaced by the mule, an animal far superior to the horse for farm work. In the past a fast-walking man with a cooperative mule could plow one side of twelve to fifteen acres of row crops per day.

—Photo courtesy of Mrs. Fanny Locklear

131

chitterlings (or "chittlins" in the spoken language). Some of the people of Robeson still have an annual chitterling feast.

As each hog came off the scaffold, it was cut into seven pieces, the head, two hams, two shoulders, and two middlings. The head was boiled in a wash pot and then ground and pressed into a fine piece of souse meat.

After the hogs were cut up the men took a break while the women started the dinner, which usually consisted of collards, corn bread, baked sweet potatoes, boiled backbone, fried lean tenderloins, and steaming hot coffee without cream or sugar. Neither milk, tea, nor desserts were prevalent on these occasions but there was always an abundance of solid and delicious food.

Following the meal, the work was resumed, the lean meat being trimmed from the hams and other pieces, then ground and stuffed into casings to make delicious sausage. The liver was boiled, ground, and mixed with "cracklins" and a seasoning of homegrown onions and sage to make pudding. Some people favored "blood pudding" which was made by adding a little of the hog blood to the ground liver. The skins were also dried. "Cracklins" and dried skin made good treats during the winter months.

The fat that was cut in the process of trimming the hog was placed in wash pots and cooked into lard, a slow process because of the danger of scorching. As the lard slowly cooked it was stirred with a green sweet bay stick which was cut from the local woods. Some of the bay leaves were put into the pot when the lard was nearly done, giving the finished product an appealing aroma.

While the lard cooked, the meat was salted down, by rubbing it vigorously with salt to achieve deep penetration. Depending on the size of the hog, the meat remained salted down from three to five weeks. At the end of the curing period, it was washed in warm water. After drying for a few minutes, borax and garden grown red pepper were sprinkled over the meat. It was then hung in the smoke house, to be enjoyed throughout the year.[2] The

---

2. Prior to the Civil War era meat was smoked to preserve it, but since the mid-nineteenth century salt has been used to accomplish this end. However, until this day the house used for storing the meat is called a "smoke house."

three M's: meat, meal, and molasses, were the staples in the Lumbee diet prior to World War II. While they no longer cure as much meat or depend as totally on their farms for vegetables as in the past, there are still some Lumbees who cling to the traditional ways.

Getting goods from the farm to the market was an awesome task in earlier times, and the Lumbees were faced with moving a variety of agricultural products, livestock, and fowl to surrounding markets in order to acquire a little necessary cash. Certainly one of the most unique farm-to-market activities engaged in by Lumbees was the driving of turkeys from the Pembroke area to Fayetteville, North Carolina, a distance of forty miles. Such a trip required several days and involved camping out under the open sky. At night, while the driver made camp, cooked his meal, and bedded down for sleep, the turkeys roosted in surrounding trees. Rising with the turkeys, the driver would continue in this way until he reached the market where he could sell his birds and then walk home, traveling at a considerably faster pace.

Woodsawings still occurred in Lumbee country as late as the 1930's. The idea of a woodsawing was to get enough men together to saw sufficient wood in three or four hours to last for a year. When the neighboring sawyers arrived, the trees had already been felled and were waiting to be cut into "stoe" (stove) and fire wood, the latter cut to fit a fireplace. Although a great deal of work was involved in a woodsawing, like so many other activities, it was also a social occasion. As the men filled the air with the sounds of work, building up huge appeties, the women began to prepare a supper to satisfy their hunger. After supper the men drank coffee or a few drams of whiskey and talked about what was going on in the community. The conversation usually concerned life on the farm, hunting trips, or fishing in the Lumbee River. Today, if a man needs wood cut for any purpose, he simply takes up his power chain saw and cuts it himself. The job might get done faster and more efficiently, but something has been definitely lost in the change from people helping people to reliance on a machine.

Other cooperative community activities among the Lumbees

were logrollings and house and barn raisings. The first involved clearing land for cultivation by cutting the trees down and then rolling the logs into big piles so they could be burned. It was an arduous task. Many of the trees reached seventy to one hundred feet into the sky and the trunks of such trees could be moved only through the concerted efforts of many strong and willing men. After the trees had been cleared out of the way, the field was cleaned of stumps and roots by men, women, and children all working together. Barn and house raisings, which were common prior to World War I, were generally completed in one day. At these affairs neighborhood men placed the heavy logs on top of each other until the building was high enough for a roof, which was later added by the owner and covered with wooden shingles. As at other such occasions, the reward was fellowship and a meal of generous proportions.

Corn shuckings also called for neighborly cooperation. In the center of a large pile of corn was a jimmy-john (jug of whiskey) which no one touched until all the corn was shucked. A few ears of red corn were usually found, which meant that the finder could kiss the girl of his choice. When all the corn was shucked, the jimmy-john was passed and the crowd danced to the music of the fiddle.

There were also activities which were strictly limited to women; for example, it was said that "the ladies took the day" at quilting parties. For several months prior to a party the woman of the house cut squares from cloth scraps, which were later sewn together in various patterns and designs to make a beautiful quilt top. Cotton, saved from the farm, was used as filler, and the seeds were often removed by hand. Many children were told in the evening that they would have to fill their shoes with cotton seeds before they could go to bed. When the day for the party arrived, the quilting frame was ready, often being suspended from the ceiling of a bedroom. The big job for the women who came to help was to sew stitches about one inch apart all over the quilt to maintain its shape and thickness. Putting the base on the edge of the quilt was usually left for the lady of the house to do during her spare time. Four experienced quilters could make two such bedcovers in a day. Lumbee women were proud of both the quality and quantity of their comforters, as evidenced by a lady of the Burnt Swamp Community who achieved her life's ambition when she was able to boast that she owned one hundred quilts.

The social opportunities of quilting are obvious, but the making of quilts was both practical and essential. Anyone who has ever lived in a house without central heat knows how cold the early hours of the morning are, once the wood or coal fire has died. The only way to keep warm under such circumstances is to have a feather bed which molds itself around you, and several quilts to spread over yourself. The contrast between the warmth of such a bed and a cold morning was never more vivid than when the rooster crowed, announcing a new day. Remembering the "good old days," one Lumbee remarked that "the minute your feet touched that cold floor you came awake. Rambling around the dark house looking for matches to start a fire in the fireplace and kitchen stove, the lazy man returned to his bed until the house got warmer, while the energetic one crawled into his clothes and went to the barn to begin his chores."

While neighbors were generous with their help for tasks requiring many hands and much strength, there were of course even more chores which the individual farmer and his family had to handle. Life on a farm was a daily round of milking, feeding, gathering, and, depending on the time of the year, of planting, cultivating or harvesting. One burdensome chore was "pulling fodder," hot and hard work done in the month of August. When the corn was mature, but most of the corn blades still green, they were pulled from the stalk. When the puller had as many as he could hold in each hand, he tied it together with two or three blades, placing the "tie" on an ear of corn. At sundown, after the fodder pulled in the morning had dried somewhat, four or five ties were bound together as a "bundle" of fodder. The bundles were then carried by hand to the end of the corn row where they were loaded on a wagon and carried to the feed barn. Fodder was fed to horses and mules but not to the cows. It was commonly believed that it would cause a milk cow to go dry. Lumbees pulled fodder primarily as an economy measure; it was cheap feed for some of the livestock and it allowed them to use most of their land to raise crops other than hay and oats.

In earlier days a typical forty-acre farmer put about half his land in money crops, such as cotton and tobacco; the remaining twenty acres were then divided as follows: fifteen acres of corn, two acres for garden vegetables and a potato patch, and three acres for hay. The hay land was used to grow two crops in a year, such as wheat, oats, or some other small grain, followed later by a crop of hay. The garden plot was used to raise white and sweet potatoes, peas, beans, okra, tomatoes, collards, turnips, cabbages, beets, and other vegetables. Small patches of sugar cane were grown, to be pressed into juice which was cooked into syrup.

Chickens were another important source of food on family farms. Generally, fifty or sixty hens were kept to insure an abundance of eggs. There was usually one rooster for every twenty hens so there would always be a supply of baby chicks. The rooster was also important as a time piece, crowing regularly and vigorously at both midnight and daybreak. "The rooster," said one Lumbee, "could be easily heard in a house that was full of cracks and holes." At times, and especially if the preacher came to dinner, a chicken would be killed and fried. On those occasions a younger member of the family would run a chicken down and an adult would wring his neck and prepare him for dinner.

While farming was the occupation of most Lumbees, a few sought livelihoods in other types of work, especially through jobs related to the lumber industry. Following the Civil War and until the early twentieth century, logs were floated down the Lumbee River into the Peedee system and on to Georgetown, South Carolina, which remains an important forest-products center to this day. The logs were tied together, forming a raft on which the men could live as they took the timber to market. Logs were moved solely by the current of the river, though the men used poles to keep them away from the banks where the shallow water would ground the rafts. It was a chance to live in the open land, to swap tales, to fight the mosquitoes and other insects that live in the swamps and swarm out during stormy weather, and to hunt and fish. If the river cooperated, the trip to Georgetown took about three weeks. Once the men reached that market, they got their few dollars and returned home on foot, a journey of more than a hundred miles.

The turpentine industry was another in which Lumbees were heavily involved. Southeastern North Carolina had been an important center for this industry prior to the Civil War, but when that conflict began, this economic activity, as well as most in the South, fell into a state of neglect. It was virtually wiped out when General William T. Sherman's Union armies entered the state in March, 1864. Although the Federals treated North Carolina far more kindly than they had South Carolina, they nevertheless did fire many of the turpentine forests, creating an incredibly beautiful spectacle of flame and smoke, but also effectively destroying an important local industry.

The economic problems of the postwar years, and especially the depressed condition of agriculture, led many Lumbees in the 1880's to migrate to other southern states. While a few went to Tennessee, Florida, and Mississippi, most went to Georgia where they became an important factor in that State's turpentine industry. The movement from Robeson was large, slow, often painful, and unfortunately did not solve all the problems the Lumbees sought to leave behind. Insecurity remained a fact of the migrants' lives, and segregation, being institutionalized throughout the South in this period, was a fact of their social and political lives.

The influence of the "Georgia experience" is shown in many ways, some obvious and some subtle. One Lumbee family, naming its children after Georgia towns, contains a Valdosta, Ozar, Savannah, Rochelle, and Cornelia. There are many stories of exploitation and misuse, of jail breaks and long flights back to Robeson, and of lost and found opportunities. Among the Lumbees who took part in this nineteenth century migration was Henry Delaware Lowrie, the son of Henry Berry Lowrie. This young man went to Mississippi where he eventually lost his life. Although the evidence is scant, it appears that Henry Delaware became involved in a quarrel with another man over a turpentine still. In the duel that followed, the two men killed each other. While a few Lumbees established permanent homes away from Robeson and apparently found contentment, most had returned by the outbreak of World War I, and were glad to be back.

When Lumbees reminisce about the past, they all generally echo the same sentiment: "Old Timers worked hard but they enjoyed life." One summed it up saying:

"It was a long, long hard day
But it was a lot of fun
Never worked too hard to say
Today is a good day to die!"

Finally, some attention must be paid to funeral customs among the Lumbees of earlier times. In the past when a man was dying, if at all possible his bed was turned to the east. People would say, "They have turned his bed for him to die."[3] After death, the body was placed on a "cooling board," to remain there until his wooden box was ready. In some instances, when the individual could bear seeing his own coffin it was made sometimes by himself years before he would use it, and stored in his barn. The coffin was usually made of good heart pine timber and would last for a great number of years. Some wooden markers made of heart pine and close to two centuries old can still be found in local cemeteries. Lumbees have never believed in rushing their dead to the grave. As a general rule, a "setting up" period of two nights was observed. The "setting up" was a social outlet for the community and a source of comfort for the bereaved. At these affairs the adults sat around the fireplace talking and chewing tobacco or using snuff. Fortunately, they could spit ten or twelve feet into hearth without ever missing a chosen spot. The young people viewed these occasions as an opportunity to do some courting. When the corpse was carried to the church for the final rites, an "old brother" would "line out" a hymn, an art made necessary by the lack of song books but still practiced among some Lumbee people.

On the whole, Lumbees attend funerals in large numbers. The biggest crowd ever to witness a funeral in Robeson County assem-

---

3. The symbolism of facing a dying man to the east has been lost, but this may well be a legacy of the Lumbees' Indian culture.

bled on a hot day in July, 1939. A young Indian had been executed in the gas chamber for a capital crime. Before his death, he requested that the local paper print his picture and a statement to the boys back home "to leave liquor alone and trust in God." An estimated four thousand people, almost all of whom were Lumbees attended the funeral either to pay their last respects or out of curiosity. While this is an extreme example, the Lumbees attach great importance to showing the family of the departed that they care and that they share their sorrow.

CONCLUSIONS

With the passage of time, the human mind has a way of weeding out the bad memories and preserving the good. As a consequence, the past always seems happier and more trouble-free than it really was. Yet, values of earlier times worth preserving unfortunately were not preserved. Among the Indians of Robeson County, there was, most of all, a sense of community born of love for one's neighbor and of necessity, a sense that gave Lumbee life a richness that could never be measured materially. Lumbee forebears were mainly concerned with making a living, and knowing some pleasure, not with becoming wealthy.

When the Lumbee "folk experience" is examined closely, it becomes obvious that their culture bears a marked similarity to that of most rural whites. While this may strike some as odd, anyone who is at all familiar with eastern Indians knows that many of them lost their native culture years ago. Numerous isolated bands, such as the "Porch Creek," point to a white cultural heritage. Certainly the Lumbees, whose relationship with Europeans goes back centuries, have every right to claim this as a legitimate legacy from the past. But notwithstanding the assimilation of the Lumbees into the white culture, they know themselves to be Indian and their heritage is enriched by both cultures. Assimilation need not, and indeed has not meant extermination for the Lumbee Indians.

Preston Locklear. A Lumbee woodsrider and member of the first Board of Trustees for the Indian Normal School.
—*Photo courtesy of Pembroke State University*

Governor Locklear. The son of Preston Locklear and the first Lumbee medical doctor, trained at The Johns Hopkins University.
—*Photo courtesy of T. B. Brayboy, Jr.*

6

A People of Hope

The coming of the twentieth century produced no sharp break with events or traditions of the past for the Lumbee Indians. Although the new century began in an atmosphere of optimism, with most Americans looking forward to a future of virtually unlimited potential and achievement, the Lumbees shared in this mood of hopeful expectation somewhat hesitantly. Their memory of the pain and suffering of the nineteenth century was still vivid. Moreover, they saw segregation being institutionalized both in the realm of politics and in social relations. Yet, the nineteenth century had produced important educational and religious gains and marked the beginning of movement toward recognition of a distinct Indian identity. In the twentieth century the Lumbees would seek to overcome the many artificial barriers which hindered their progress and equality.

During the transitional years from the nineteenth to the twentieth century, the Lumbee central town of Pembroke was founded, largely a product of the present but with strong roots in the past. As Eugene M. Musselwhite points out in his informative example of local history, *The "Iron Horse" Comes to Robeson*, Pembroke township owes its origin to the railroads. Originally, the site of Pembroke was known as Campbell's Mill, situated on

Watering Hole Swamp and complete with a large pond extending in a southeasterly direction. In 1860 the Wilmington, Charlotte and Rutherfordton Railroad, the first line in Robeson County, was built on a trestle across the mill pond at that location. However, there is no evidence that either a railroad station or a post office existed there until years later. Indeed, the most important communities in the area at the time were Moss Neck, located a few miles east of Campbell's Mill and Pates, situated a few miles to the west. Moss Neck, as indicated earlier, originated as a turpentine distilling center and maintained that activity until the pine forests were depleted and the industry moved south. It was saved from extinction because it had a cooperage firm and a post office and it enjoyed a brief resurgence when the railroad established a station there. Pates was established around 1880 by Russell W. Livermore, who originally came into the area to settle the estate of a deceased friend, liked what he saw, and stayed. Pates had approximately one hundred inhabitants by 1884, and had become a railroad station and the center of Livermore's thriving mercantile and farming operations.

Apparently Moss Neck and Pates prevented any real community from developing at Campbell's Mill until 1892. In that year the Wilmington and Weldon Railroad wanted to build its so-called "Wilson Shortcut" through Moss Neck, but met opposition from a prominent citizen in the area, and therefore it moved its north-south line to Campbell's Mill, where it intersected the already existing east-west line.[1] As a consequence, a railroad station was established and a community began to grow. The Atlantic Land and Improvement Company laid the town out in a one-mile square with streets, blocks, and lots. The center of town was to be the crossing of the railroads. Once the community had been laid out, the land was sold or given to private owners. The town was incorporated by an act of the legislature in 1895 and it quickly became a trading center for the surrounding area, receiving an added boost when the Normal School was moved to the vicinity in 1909. How the new community acquired the name of Pembroke is dis-

1. The railroads serving the area have undergone numerous name changes but today they are all part of the Seaboard Coastline system.

142

puted. A few people believe that it was named after the British town of Pembroke, but the great majority say it was named after Pembroke Jones, a railway official, and the evidence points to the latter explanation.

When Pembroke was incorporated in 1895, the citizens of the town were allowed to elect annually a mayor and four commissioners. In an age of segregation and political disfranchisement, the whites, though a minority, controlled the municipal government. This arrangement prevailed until 1917. By that year the composition of the town's population had become overwhelmingly Indian, and they began to demand a voice in the town government. Since the white establishment opposed this, they sent a group to Raleigh and obtained the legislature's help in changing the method by which town officials were chosen. Under the new procedure which was worked out, the governor appointed the mayor and the commissioners, thus insuring white control of the municipal government for the next thirty years. However, from the beginning and apparently as the result of a gentleman's agreement, Indians served on the commission. In time, the municipal government came to consist of two Indian commissioners, two white commissioners, and a white mayor. In 1945, a group of Lumbees went to the governor and asked that the citizens be allowed to elect their officials in a democratic manner. According to local sources, the governor consulted the three most influential whites in Pembroke as to how they felt on the matter and when they replied favorably, he granted the Indians' request for democracy. The fact that the governor was mainly concerned with the white reaction, not with the will of the majority, says a great deal about prevailing attitudes and policies.

Since 1947, when the revised political process took effect, there have been five mayors of Pembroke, all Lumbees. The first Indian to be elected mayor was Reverend Clarence E. Locklear; the other four were J. C. Oxendine, Samuel Locklear, Earlie Maynor, and Juddie Revels. The first four were Democrats, the last a Republican. Presently, the entire municipal government is made up of Lumbees. This is not surprising, since the town's population is predominantly Indian.

Pembroke appeared much like a western town in the early twentieth century. It was made up of wooden buildings with shelters across their fronts and dirt sidewalks. The first brick building was constructed in 1922. The first highway through Pembroke was opened in 1923, paralleling the east-west railroad track. The first concrete street was built in 1932 by private property owners and is now East Main Street. At the present time, Pembroke has between twelve and fifteen miles of streets, most of which are paved.

According to tradition, Thaggard's, McCormick's, and Breece's were the first stores in the town. As a representative example of an early merchant Gus Thaggard was a man of varied interests; he ran a hotel, a general store, a livery stable, and the post office. Interestingly, Mr. Thaggard was a Democrat while his wife was a Republican. In an age when postmasterships were patronage positions, the fact that they were of different political affiliations allowed them to keep control of the post office regardless of which party was in power.

The largest store in Pembroke is Pates Supply Company, organized as a partnership between Z. V. Pate, Hugh Monroe, and Russell H. Livermore in the early 1920's. This was a general store supplying credit to farmers in return for liens against their crops. While such an arrangement no doubt enabled many farmers to make it from year to year, it also meant that they specialized too heavily in staples, such as tobacco and cotton, and that they stood to lose their lands if they experienced too many crop failures over a period of time. Fortunately for most local farmers, Pate's was operated honestly. Property was taken through foreclosures only when unavoidable.

Not all general merchants, however, dealt with the local farmers as fairly at Pates. Because few Lumbee farmers had any formal education in the early years of this century, and because they failed to understand the need to keep records, most were constantly in debt. Thus, at "settling" time, it was easy for a dishonest merchant to take advantage of the farmer's ignorance and keep him in debt or take his land. Many Lumbee farmers tell the story of how they paid for their farm more than once. There are also many bitter memories in the Lumbee community of how some lawyers acquired land as payment for representing Indians in court, and how some lawyers used the tax laws to their advantage, particularly during the Great Depression. As Lumbee farmers acquired education, the situation changed. They began to keep records and receipts, and to demand their rights.

Today, Pembroke has the appearance of any small town in America serving a predominantly rural population. Most of the buildings are brick; there are stores offering a variety of goods and services; there is even a modern shopping center. The town government is responsible for providing police and fire protection, sewage and water service, all of which have been improved over the past few years, with the help of various federal programs. In addition, a number of public housing units have been constructed as a step toward improving the quality of life in the area. While there are a number of new industries in the county, and Indians are an important part of the work force in most of them, there are only a few small industries within Pembroke itself, including a small Indian-owned garment plant and a mobile home factory.

Pembroke has known a slow but steady growth in population since it was incorporated in 1895. From approximately one hundred and fifty people in the mid-1890's, the population has grown to about 1,800 in 1974. However, approximately 5,000 people live within a radius of two miles of the town. Of the present population, 88 percent is Indian, 8 percent white, and 4 percent Negro. The small Negro population no doubt reflects the fact that the Indians owned few slaves in the ante-bellum period. After the Civil War, the black people were kept out because of white attempts to force Indians into the same status as the freedmen.

Pembroke had a fairly high crime rate in the past, especially in the incidence of crimes of violence. This was a product of the frontier-like environment of the rather isolated area around Pembroke, as well as of ignorance, frustration, and, in some cases, liquor. Most crimes were committed by Indians against Indians. It was general practice, that if an Indian killed another Indian it was second degree murder, but if an Indian killed a white, it was first degree murder. Today, Pembroke's crime rate is much like that of any small town. An effective police force has been established. More and more of the citizens have acquired values which demand order and security. Pembroke's progress is rightfully a source of pride for the Indians of Robeson County, despite the problems and issues.

Although Pembroke rapidly became the focal point for Lumbee business activities, the Indians themselves remained basically a rural people. Whereas cotton was the predominent staple in the nineteenth century, beginning in the 1890's tobacco increasingly replaced it as the area's principal money crop. This change occurred primarily because the price of cotton was low during the nineties, dropping to five cents per pound in 1898; never rising over ten cents a pound during the decade. Since a farmer needed at least seven cents a pound to break even, the raising of cotton was a money-losing or low-profit operation at best. Cotton further declined as the dreaded boll weevil spread northward, reaching the Lumbee area by the 1920's. Only with the introduction of effective insecticides in recent years has cotton culture revived in the South, and increasing demand for this product seems likely. As cotton underwent its years of decline, tobacco boomed and continues to be an extremely important crop for all farmers in southeastern North Carolina. The planting, cultivation and harvesting, curing, and marketing of tobacco demanded more time and skills than did cotton production, but the Lumbees quickly mastered these skills and became among the best tobacco farmers in the nation.

In earlier days "going to market" to sell the cured leaf was both a business and social occasion. Tobacco is sold in large warehouses from July to October. During the selling season a market town acquires an exciting atmosphere and distinctive aroma, both of which were more pronounced before warehouse operations became formal and reasonably efficient. Until the 1950's farmers brought their tobacco to town by whatever means they had, with many still relying on the mule and wagon, and they remained in town until their leaf was sold. The tobacco season was a time of prosperity for local businessmen, but especially for those who operated cafes, clothing stores, and hotels. While the tobacco season remains an important economic factor, the success or failure of a business year is not totally dependent upon it, as in the past. Tourism and corporations have become year-round sources of income and farmers can now sell quickly and get home easily. That tobacco continues to be an important part of the economy is seen in the fact that local markets annually sell over 100 million pounds of the golden leaf, at steadily rising prices. The 1973 crop brought an acreage price of 88 cents per pound and the projected average for 1974 was 95 cents. Such prices were inconceivable a decade ago. But the cost of raising tobacco, as in the case of all crops, has been rising due largely to the higher costs of fertilizer, insecticide, fuel, and labor. Still, the basic rule of thumb is that a farmer, with a little cooperation from nature, should be able to gross $1,500 per acre on tobacco, and most do.

Three of the more noteworthy agricultural developments in Lumbee country have been the increasing diversification of agriculture, the acceptance of scientific methods, and the decline in tenant farming. More Lumbees own land today than at any time since the coming of the European settlers in the 1730's. They have begun to raise other money crops on an extensive scale, such as soybeans, cucumbers, tomatoes and green peppers, as well as more livestock for the market. Finally, Lumbee farmers have become more knowledgeable in the methods for increasing productivity and maintaining soil fertility, and concerning the many and varied government programs that affect farming. Most Lumbees readily concede that success in farming today depends almost as much on knowledge as on skill and experience.

While the agrarians of today are on the whole superior to their predecessors, the Lumbees have always been good farmers. One of the more outstanding was Sim Bullard of the Prospect Community. Bullard owned a large farm which his family had cleared and fenced and on which, in addition to the standard implements, he had his own cotton gin and sawmill. The work day began early in the Bullard household, breakfast was served before daylight. All ate heartily in preparation for walking a dozen head of mules at a fast pace, up and down every row of cotton. One mule could sweep (plow) fifteen acres of cotton and "leave the

147

Taking tobacco to market—the way it was. Farmers line up to get into the warehouse to unload their valuable leaf. In past days "going to market" was both a social and economic occasion.

—Photo courtesy of THE ROBESONIAN

Out of the past. As late as the 1930's the mule-drawn wagon was a familiar sight behind stores, on the roads, and in the fields of Robeson County.

—Photo by William P. Revels

sun running." Of course, the hardest job was getting the cotton out of the field. Picking cotton was slow, backbreaking work even for fast workers. Any man or woman who could pick three hundred or more pounds in a day was in great demand at picking time. There were a few workers who could pick five hundred pounds in a day, but they were a rarity. During that period, the whole family went to the fields, where the infants slept under the cotton stalks and the older children, from five to six and up, were given tasks to perform. Many small children could pick one hundred pounds of cotton in a day. Since farming was the whole family's business, anyone who failed to do his part could expect to be punished, either with sarcastic criticism or, in some cases, by a whipping with cotton stalks. Such punishment usually produced greater efficiency the next day. Cotton was picked in tow sacks and emptied into tow sheets. Six good sheets full of cotton made a bale weighing approximately 1,500 pounds. When the cotton was ginned (the seed separated from the lint), this amount would produce a bale of more than 500 pounds. Sim Bullard, having his own cotton gin, was more fortunate than most small farmers who traveled eight to ten miles daily to get their cotton to the gin. When Bullard sold cotton, he borrowed all the mules and wagons in his vicinity. "It was," said one old Lumbee, "an impressive sight to see a mule train a mile long carrying Mr. Sim's cotton to market."

When the United States became involved in the First World War in 1917, there was no reluctance on the part of the government to take Lumbees as soldiers. The majority who served were given their basic training at Camp Jackson, South Carolina. For many Lumbees this was their first experience away from home, and they still laugh at the story of the sergeant who was checking the roster at reveille and called out "Locklear, John," to which the young Indian naively responded, "Sergeant, you called my name backwards." The Sergeant's reaction was predictable. He said, "We'll have no more damn wisecracks out of you." When the training process was over, these raw recruits had become top-flight soldiers. Lumbees tell with pride of how the company commander addressed his outfit and, calling each Lumbee by name, said, "I

Top. Mrs. Josephine Smith. One of thousands of Lumbee ladies who help make Robeson County a leading tobacco growing area. Barn in background is used for curing tobacco, a process requiring heating interior of barn to temperature of 180 to 190 degrees.

Bottom. Cropping tobacco. This is a hot job in July and August.

—*Photo courtesy of Elmer Hunt*

had rather go overseas with these Indians than a whole battalion of you white fellows."

True to their tradition of serving in the nation's armed forces, a tradition that dates back to the Revolution, these Indians went to France where thirteen were killed. Yet, remarkably, the Indian people reflect no bitterness about participation in this or any other of the white man's wars. They accept service as a duty and choose instead to remember the humor of what was a heart rending time for some. For example, Abner Locklear was one of the Indians who served in World War I. Somehow the word got out that Abner had been killed and that his body would arrive at the Red Banks depot on a given day at a stated time. Friends and relatives were at the station with a two-horse wagon to receive the body and were pleasantly shocked when Abner himself got off the train. When told that he was supposed to be dead and that the crowd was there to honor him and to see that he was decently buried, Abner jokingly said, "I'm mighty sorry you all got disappointed."

The Lumbee veterans who returned from the war found that little had changed during their absence. Segregation and discrimination still dominated the local society; farming remained practically the only economic activity open to them. While the decade of the 'twenties is generally depicted as a time of gaiety and prosperity ("the roaring twenties"), most Americans, and especially the farmers, found it to be neither exciting nor prosperous. Agriculture experienced a sharp depression once the war had ended, and the European market had been lost. It never fully recovered under the business-oriented administrations of the 1920's. Lumbee farmers suffered from the low prices, limited markets, and high tariffs, just as their counterparts did in the rest of the nation. When the stock market crashed in 1929 signaling the onset of the Great Depression, the Lumbees felt its effects, but not as acutely as most other Americans. The Lumbees owned no stock, and so did not worry unduly about the collapse of the market. But the depression which followed, with its massive unemployment and dislocations, further intensified the agricultural problems that already existed. Prices dropped even lower, credit became difficult to find, and the loss of one's lands became a distinct possibility. Unfortunately, the Lumbees, like all farmers, responded to their worsening economic situation with increased productivity, which only pushed prices lower. However, no matter how bad conditions became, the Lumbee farmers managed to eat well because of their excellent vegetable gardens and livestock.

For those Lumbees who were not farmers, the depression meant taking whatever job was available, including those provided under various New Deal programs such as the Works Progress Administration. It was not unusual in those times to work for fifty cents per day, or to hire out as a farm hand for six to eight dollars a month. A few people even hired out for room, board, and clothing. Although times were difficult and money almost nonexistent, the Lumbees amused themselves in this period with sandlot baseball, hunting, fishing, or just visiting the neighbors for some friendly conversation.

The depression led the federal government to undertake several interesting experiments in Robeson County. In 1936 the United States government appropriated $850,000 for a resettlement project for the Lumbee Indians. Land was bought, primarily from white citizens of the county. The old buildings were razed; new houses and barns were built. The farms were fenced and money was made available for buying livestock. Every farm had chickens. In short, each farm and farmhouse was to be a small model operation. Loans for purchasing the farms were made for forty years, although short-term financing was available for those who could manage it.

The big criticism of this farm operation was that it took too long to pay off the loans. The farmers felt they would never own the land which they were working. Today, all the farms have drifted into other hands. Most of the land is still owned by Indians, but they operate the same as any other farmer, without interference from the federal government. Only a few of the buildings constructed in the 1930's remain. Many of the frame houses have been replaced by modern brick homes. The Indians have learned to take advantage of the various government programs available for financing houses, and the appearance of the countryside has been changing.

Separate from the Resettlement Project was a cooperative farm plan organized as the Red Banks Mutual Association. A 1,600-acre parcel of land, part of the old Red Banks plantation, was purchased from the Fletcher Brothers of South Carolina. Every building on the property was torn down except the big house where the overseer lived. Two large barns were built to house a few dozen mules and for storage of animal feed. Each family participating in this experiment received a small farm house, a smoke house, and a chicken house. The idea of this farmers' cooperative was for all the participants to work together and share the profits. Adults and children were paid hourly wages for their work on the farm during the year. Then, if there were profits at the end of the year, they were divided equally among the members of the Red Banks Mutual Association.

The Red Banks project continued its existence into the 1960's; but as an experiment in communal living it was not successful. From the beginning there was great suspicion among the Lumbees as to the government's intentions. Some believed that this was the first step toward forcing them onto a reservation. Even bigger problems were the individualism of the people and their acceptance of private property, not having owned lands in common since the early eighteenth century. Morover, the wages paid were very low (a pittance of thirty cents an hour in 1957), and there were management problems. Finally, after the depression years passed, Congress seemed to lose interest in experiments of this nature and inadequate funding contributed to its collapse.

When the project finally folded, the government gave the members of the Red Banks Mutual Association an opportunity to buy the land. One of the requirements for purchase was that the land a farmer bought must contain a decent house. Several of the participants shrewdly built a new house, acquired title to the land, and then sold a portion of it to pay off their debts. Notably, few Lumbees regret the failure of this experiment in land reform.

One positive development resulting from the Red Banks project was the Lumbee Recreation Center. Funded through paid memberships and one-half million dollars from the Farm Home Administration, 376 acres of the cooperative's lands were purchased and used for the construction of an eighteen-hole golf course, swimming pool, fish pond, lighted ball park, and several other smaller facilities. Although the project ultimately proved too costly for its members to maintain and has now passed to private ownership, it still exists as a recreation center. Many Lumbees hoped that the state would buy it and make it available as a park for all the people, but the General Assembly of North Carolina declined to do so.

By the late 1930's it was becoming clear that the Fascist states were a threat to world peace, and with the outbreak of war in 1939 the United States began to prepare itself psychologically and physically for war. In 1941, when this country was drawn into the spreading conflict, Lumbee youths were once again called to the aid of their country. The Indians of Robeson served with distinction and courage in all parts of the Armed Forces. Many were decorated for gallantry in action. At least forty died for a country that had not accepted them as first-class citizens for more than a century. They would continue to do so in places such as Korea and Vietnam, because this was still their land and they believed in the ideals of America. Indeed, few people celebrate July the Fourth as joyously as do the Lumbee Indians. Today, they combine that national holiday with Lumbee Homecoming and the atmosphere is that of a great family reunion, a political meeting, and a revival, all rolled into one.

Although World War II brought sadness to some and pride to many, it also brought social change to southeastern North Carolina and the Lumbees. Pembroke was within forty miles of two major military installations during the war, the Laurinburg-Maxton Air Base and Fort Bragg. Lumbee girls are among the most beautiful to be seen anywhere, and soldiers with week-end passes soon filled the streets of the town. In remembering how it was in those days, one Lumbee remarked that "Love is like the dew, it will fall anywhere as quick as it falls on a rose; that is what happened to Lumbee girls, they married white." Lumbee servicemen likewise took non-Indian wives. Also, some Indians from other parts of the country, brought into the area by the military, married into the Lumbee community. Much of the provincialism and isolation of the Lumbees was destroyed in the crucible of war.

The end of the depression and the coming of war caused many Lumbees to head for the city to look for work. Baltimore and Detroit received the greatest share of Indians from Robeson County. The first was only three hundred miles from home and the second offered almost certain employment. In addition, Lumbees like to follow Lumbees. This migratory trend which began in the late 1930's was greatly accelerated in the post-war years. One Lumbee explained his decision to move to the city by saying: "After I returned from World War II, I decided to go away and look for a job. I knew a Lumbee friend in Baltimore who was gainfully employed. At home I could compete with this Lumbee friend; therefore, I felt that I could be just as successful in Baltimore as he." The lack of jobs at home joined with this kind of logic propelled many Lumbees into the city.

Today, there are approximately 4,000 Lumbees living in Baltimore. However, according to Herbert Locklear, founder and director of the American Indian Center in that city:

> We still call Robeson County home. Unlike many other Americans who are drawn to the city by its exciting opportunities, most American Indians come only because they are desperate. Therefore, instead of 'coming' to something, they are 'leaving' something to find work. There is simply nothing for them back home. They do not like the crowds, the traffic, or the constant pressure of city life; most would return to their home if stable employment were available for them there.

Most of the Lumbees in Baltimore who go to church attend the West Cross Street Baptist Church. The congregation is nearly one hundred percent Lumbee, with a Lumbee pastor, James M. Dial. Unlike most of his congregation, Dial finds Baltimore a good place in which to live and says he expects to make it his home. He has adjusted to the competitive, aggressive pace of urban life better than most.

Although some scholars question his findings, Professor Mohammod Amanullah in his study *The Lumbee Indians: Patterns of Adjustment* drew the following conclusions concerning the

Lumbees in Baltimore: (1) most live in rental apartments; (2) approximately one-third are on welfare; (3) Lumbee parents are generally permissive and yet use harsh punishment; (4) parents outwardly place high value on education but do not check to see that their children do their best; (5) the majority of Lumbee children attend school No. 27 which has been called the worst in the city system; (6) Lumbees believe in marrying within their own race; (7) Lumbees don't approve of divorce but agree to that course of action when a marriage isn't working; (8) Lumbees feel a sense of insecurity, anxiety, hostility, and suspicion; and (9) religion is an integral part of Lumbee life. What Amanullah discovered through his research is what most Lumbees already knew: that cities hold problems as well as promise and that if they had a choice, they would rather be somewhere else, preferably back home. Significantly, the situation has begun to change at home, to the extent that whereas some Lumbee parents encourage their children to leave North Carolina in the past, today, despite various problems, almost all Lumbees agree that "Lumbee country is beautiful."

Although World War II began to weaken racial barriers and to broaden the horizons of non-white veterans, many of the practices and traditions of the past yielded to change only grudgingly. This was especially true of the institution of segregation. A Lumbee veteran who served in the European theater during the war recalled an incident of prejudice shortly after his return home.

> I went to a square dance in a neighboring town with some Indian and white friends. As I stood in line to get tickets, a policeman looked me over. He finally walked up to me and asked, 'Are you Indian?', to which I proudly replied yes. He then said, 'Well, you can't go in.' I turned and walked away, followed by my friends who had joined me for an evening of fun. Although no one mentioned the incident as we drove back to Pembroke; it gave me a strange feeling. I couldn't help but wonder how I could be free everywhere except at home.

The disappointment and frustration experienced by the young veteran was shared by other Lumbees. Prior to 1954, "Jim Crow" signs appeared everywhere in Robeson except in Pembroke. Public restrooms were marked *white, Indian,* and *Negro.* Water fountains were designated by race. Public accommodations, such as restaurants, were segregated. However, beginning in the late 1940's under President Harry S. Truman, the federal government reluctantly began to pay some attention to the civil rights issue, thus setting the stage for the landmark *Brown Decision* of 1954. In that historic case the Warren Court ruled that:

> In the field of public education, the doctrine of separate but equal has no place. Separate educational facilities are inherently unequal. Therefore, we hold that the plaintiffs and others similarly situated for whom the actions have been brought are, by reason of the segregation complained of, deprived of the equal protection of the laws guaranteed by the Fourteenth Amendment.

Lumbees, like other ethnic peoples, considered this a major step forward in civil rights, though the fight for equality has not ended. It is difficult to visualize the Lumbee people as "a minority," when they constitute the great majority of the population in their town, a town they founded, maintained, cherished, and loved.

Paralleling the human-rights movement was a movement among the Indians of Robeson County to acquire a name for themselves that would convey pride and have permanence and dignity. This movement was spearheaded by Rev. D. F. Lowry, a prominent community leader. Meetings were held and those who favored a new name chose "Lumbee" after the river that flowed through their lands. A committee was chosen to present this name to the legislature. A bill was drawn and debated, and the Indian people were instructed to hold an election to determine popular will. This course of action was taken because there was initially considerable opposition to the idea of yet another name. Under the rules established for this election the balloting was to occur on February 2, 1952. All Indians 21 years of age and over were eligible to vote. Polling places were established at Indian schools for convenience, and a simple majority would determine the wishes of the people concerning the proposed name. Although the voter turnout was light, the ratio was approximately sixty to one

Hayes Pond. It was across this pond in a barren field, near Maxton, North Carolina, that the Lumbee Indians broke up a Ku Klux Klan rally on January 18, 1958. As a result of this affair, the Lumbees made international news.

—Photo by William P. Revels

in favor of the name "Lumbee." The Indians in adjoining counties did not vote, but they too appeared to be solidly behind this change. Once the will of the people was known, the North Carolina General Assembly, in 1953, passed a law officially designating them as the *Lumbee Indians.* The United States Congress followed suit in 1956.

The Lumbee name gained national attention in 1958 with the unintentional assistance of the Ku Klux Klan. On January 13, 1958, crosses were burned in the front yards of two Indian families. The fiery crosses, according to Lumbees, were to frighten an Indian family that had recently moved into a white neighborhood and to frighten an Indian woman accused of going with a white man. James W. "Catfish" Cole, a Grand Wizard of the Klan from Marion, South Carolina, stated publicly in the aftermath of the burnings, "I am for segregation." Cole, a self-styled preacher, then announced plans to hold a rally in Robeson County "to put the Indians in their place, to end race-mixing." The Klan attempted to lease a site in or near Pembroke for their meeting, but the Lumbees made certain no such land was available. The KKK was forced to look elsewhere; it finally found and leased a field ten miles from Pembroke near Maxton, North Carolina. The rally was set for Saturday night, January 18, 1958. Because the Lumbees were visibly aroused by the Klan's attempts at intimidation and its white supremacist attitudes, Malcolm McLeod, the sheriff of Robeson County, tried to dissuade Cole and his followers from their plans. The sheriff's warning of possible danger was ignored.

At twilight on January 18, Klansmen began to arrive for their gathering, but so did hundreds of Lumbee Indians. Both groups were armed. Charles Craven, a reporter for the Raleigh *News and Observer,* described the setting.

> Darkness had descended. It was freezing cold. The cars kept coming. The Klansmen had set up headquarters in the center of the field. They had stretched a huge banner emblazoned with KKK and had erected a long pole with a naked light bulb on it. Religious music blared forth on the cold air from a public address system. The Indians were arriving in fours and sixes and were getting from their cars and lining along the road. The

armed Klansmen were at the little circle of cars in the center of the field and some patrolled at the edges of the darkness. Some of the young Indians along the road had begun laughing and shouting, giving war whoops. Now and again somebody would yell, 'God Damn the Ku Klux Klan.'

Sheriff McLeod was at the scene with several deputies. He told the Klan leader, "Well, you know how it is. I can't control the crowd with the few men I've got. I'm not telling you not to hold a meeting, but you see how it is. You've leased the land and have a right to be here, but you see how it is." Then, suddenly, a scuffle began over the one light, between several Indian youths and a Klansman trying to protect it. A shot was fired into the air, the light was broken, and the tension was shattered by the roar of guns and shouting. The sheriff radioed the highway patrol for help and within minutes peace was restored. But the Klan had been routed and the Lumbees were jubilant. Miraculously, given the circumstances and conditions, no one was seriously injured.

Cole and James Martin, a fellow Klansman, were indicted for inciting a riot. Martin was tried in the Maxton Recorder's Court with Lacy Maynor, a Lumbee, presiding. Martin was convicted and Judge Maynor lectured him prior to sentencing. Among his comments the Lumbee jurist said: "You came into a community with guns, where there was a very happy and contented group of people. We don't go along with violence. . . We can't understand why you want to come here and bring discord." Maynor then gave the Klansman six to twelve months in prison. Cole had to be extradited from South Carolina and was tried in the Robeson County Superior Court in March, 1958. He too was convicted and sentenced to eighteen to twenty-four months imprisonment. After his trial, Cole told a reporter, "The action of the court in Robeson County has done more to prove in three and a half days than I have by my preaching in eight years that this country is fast falling into communism and dictatorship."

Among the Lumbees who received special recognition for breaking up the Klan rally was Sim Oxendine, a veteran of the Second World War and an operator of a service station in Pembroke. Oxendine said of the affair, "We called a meeting at the

Top. This one-room school, now restored as a reminder of the past, was an Indian school serving the children who lived within walking distance of it. Typically, such a school had a wood-burning stove, long seats, and a shelf filled with lunches packed in paper bags and lard buckets.

—Photo by William P. Revels

Center. The Indian State Normal campus in the mid-1920's.

—Photo courtesy of Elmer Hunt

Bottom. Prospect School (c. 1930). An all-Indian public school in Robeson County.

—Photo courtesy of Elmer Hunt

Town Hall—just a few people—and decided to let the Klan make the first move." According to Oxendine, Cole had once come to Pembroke with a small tent for a revival but had to leave because there was no interest in his message. "He did not like it because the Indians would not attend and he never did forgive them." Of his part in ending the Klan rally, Oxendine said, "I helped to pull the Klan's flag down and this seemed to make them mad. When the light was shot out, lots of shooting, running, and yelling took place." A photograph showing Oxendine wrapped in the Klan flag brought him international attention. He received more than two thousand letters, telegrams, and cablegrams from all the states and eight foreign countries, including Russia. He was invited to New York to appear on television with his father, J. C. Oxendine, who was mayor of Pembroke at the time; and he was made an honorary life member of the Pawnee tribe. In assessing the importance of the Lumbees' victory over the Klan, Oxendine commented: "We killed the Klan once and for all. We did the right thing for all people."

Although the fight against the Klan was the most spectacular event involving Lumbees in the 1950's, there was another less-noticeable development that promised genuine progress. In 1955 Early Bullard was elected judge of the Maxton Recorder's Court, thus becoming the first Lumbee ever to sit on the bench at any level in Robeson County. His election signaled growing Lumbee interest in politics. The Lumbees had come to realize that political power was another avenue to change, that everything could not be accomplished through economics and education. The Lumbees, as noted earlier, were aided in their political growth by outside help from such agencies as the American Friends Service Committee and the United Methodist Church. Yet, in the final analysis, it was their own awareness that the situation in Robeson could be improved and their cognizance that politics was an instrument for orderly change that led them to adopt their own version of the policy of self-determination.

Political consciousness caused an increasing number of Lumbees to seek public office and a growing number have been winning election and gaining appointments.[2] Lumbees have been serving on the Robeson County Board of Commissioners which administers the county's affairs, on the county board of education, in the sheriff's department, in the tax office, on the board of elections, and one young Lumbee representative has been elected to the state legislature. In addition, a number of Lumbees have been holding federal appointments. Using the "American way," Lumbees have been gaining influence and making their presence felt.

At the start of the 1970's most Lumbees believed that the question of a name for the people had been permanently decided. Such was not the case, however. Dissatisfaction arose among a group of Indians who said the name "Lumbee" had no historical meaning. They organized themselves into the Eastern Carolina Indian Organization (ECIO) — a grassroots movement — and waged an aggressive campaign to achieve two basic objectives. First, they wanted national recognition as Tuscarora Indians, and second, they wanted Indian schools controlled by Indian people. In the formative stages of their campaign they were largely ignored by the inhabitants and authorities of Robeson County. Using militant tactics, they were soon heard locally and nationally. In 1972, the ECIO under the colorful leadership of Carnell Locklear, Howard Brooks, and others, brought some sleepless nights to the people of Robeson County. Speaking out, Locklear said, "We came prepared to give our lives. . . Viet Nam is not the longest war in this nation's history. The war with the American Indian is the longest war. . . We want the United States to know we will not stand for even one American Indian to be brutalized."

The organization brought Indians to Robeson County who had won national prominence and Indians whose names are now synonymous with "The Trail of Broken Treaties" and the "Second Battle of Wounded Knee." Among those who came were Dennis Banks and Vernon Bellecourt of the American Indian Movement (AIM). When Banks spoke to a cheering crowd of two hundred Indians who had gathered on the grounds of the Robeson County Board of Education, he said, "Eleven thousand Indians are on their way to Washington, but the crisis may not be in Washing-

2. For a list of Lumbees involved in national Indian affairs, see Appendix C. For a list of those holding public office, see Appendix D.

Top. Judge Lacy W. Maynor. A Lumbee judge during the Ku Klux
Klan episode of 1958.

—Photo courtesy of Mrs. Sally Maynor

Bottom. Herbert G. Oxendine. A former dean of Pembroke State University, a civil leader, and one of the most respected members of the
Lumbee community, "a man who loved and worked for others."

—Photo courtesy of Deborah Oxendine Sampson

ton. This is a day bringing an end to the white man's rule, the new day is tomorrow at nine o'clock when we charge into the Robeson County Board of Education and confront those people who have been robbing the Indians of their heritage." Speaking of the integrated schools that had come to Robeson County, Banks said, "I favor Indians having their own schools." Notably, most Lumbees disagreed with Banks on this subject, preferring quality education to segregated schools. However, the Tuscarora faction agreed with the Indian leader. Banks continued, "It's no longer a question of whether we're going to take our schools back, it's a matter of when." After a conference with local, state, and national officials, which gave them no satisfaction, several car loads of the Tuscaroras left Robeson County to join the Indians in Washington who had made the journey called the "Trail of Broken Treaties." When the Bureau of Indian Affairs building was taken over by the Indians, the Tuscaroras played a role in the action. Several months after the BIA takeover, law enforcement officials found four tons of BIA records in an abandoned farm house in Robeson County. Two Tuscaroras, Keever Locklear and Dock Locklear, Jr., and an AIM leader, William Frederick Sargent, were indicted by a federal grand jury on charges of unlawfully, willingly and knowingly receiving and concealing property from the BIA. The Locklears were also charged with threatening four FBI agents who directed the seizure of the documents. The so-called "records case" was tried in Wilmington, North Carolina in December, 1973. After eight days of testimony, the jury deliberated for less than an hour and acquitted all three of the charges. One source stated that the jury made that decision because there was no proof of intent to commit a crime.

The Tuscaroras have also persistently challenged the local board of education concerning a grant of $487,000 given Robeson County under the Indian Education Act. They maintain that all of the funds should be used for their benefit on the grounds that they are the only "legal" Indians in the area. But even greater than their concern that the Lumbees might share the money was their belief that it was being used for all children and for frivolous purposes. The Tuscaroras asserted they would like to have such grants used to give them a language of their own; the Lumbees stated they prefer to see monies of that sort used for more practical purposes.

Regardless of the justice or logic of their position, the Tuscaroras and AIM did introduce an element of militancy into the Indian community. As a result, there were night caravans, confrontations with school officials and "the law," and a march on Raleigh, the state capital. While it may have been coincidental, Robeson County also experienced a series of fires in late 1972 and 1973. More than forty buildings burned during that time and arson was suspected in the case of most. Of all the fires in North Carolina's history, none brought as many tears, filled as many pages, and produced as many new politicians as the fire which destroyed the building known as "Old Main" on the Pembroke State University campus.

Prior to being ravaged by fire on Sunday, March 18, 1973, Old Main had become an emotional and political issue of local, state, and national prominence. Even more, it had come to symbolize for the Lumbee Indians their past experiences and opportunities, and their future hopes. The furor over Old Main began some months earlier, when Pembroke State University officials announced that the building would be demolished and its site used for the construction of a new $1.6 million auditorium. As this news spread through the community, a growing number of Lumbees began to voice protests on the grounds that Old Main represented the last physical evidence of the years when Pembroke State served only Indians. Funded in 1921 and completed in 1923, Old Main came into existence as a result of segregation laws, but by 1973 the people looked upon it as a monument to their progress and successes. It had become a vital part of Lumbee history, and a source of pride.

As opposition to the demolition of the building grew, a "Save-Old-Main" movement began. The movement originated with the Lumbee Regional Development Association (LRDA), a community action organization with a broad base of programs in areas such as adult basic education, economic development, and talent search. Danford Dial, associated with LRDA at the time, was one of the early guiding forces in the "Save-Old-Main" effort. But the movement quickly spread and attracted Lumbees who had no ties with LRDA and gained the support, as well, of other Native Americans. One of the most vigorous spokesmen in behalf of saving the historic structure was Brantly Blue, the first Lumbee to earn a law degree, a Republican, and a member of the federal Indian Claims Commission. In a letter to the *Robesonian,* a local paper, Commissioner Blue stressed the ties between the Indian people and Old Main and concluded with the remark: "Perhaps we are losing too much of our heritage; I join the club, 'Save Old Main'." He expressed the sentiment of many other Lumbees. Dozens of letters and speeches followed, stressing the importance of preserving this part of the Lumbee past and offering suggestions for the future use of Old Main, such as making it into an Indian cultural center and museum.

When the Old Main controversy began, the university administration was silent on the issue for several days. Then, Chancellor English Jones stated his understanding of the situation. He said:

> The money for Old Main, $75,000, was appropriated in 1921 by the state legislature. That building was contracted and built by paid labor like every other facility on this campus which is owned by the state. Therefore, the building has always been owned by the state of North Carolina. . . and the local people have had no more in it than the people of any other county. . . who have been taxpayers and contribute to the general fund of the state.

Dr. Jones went on to say that he did not want to see the university lose its new auditorium to preserve Old Main.

While some Lumbees squarely backed the Chancellor, most said they wanted both Old Main and the auditorium. The days that followed were filled with meetings and rallies. A petition urging that the building be saved was circulated and 7,000 people signed it. Proposals and counter-proposals were made. Republican and Democratic politicians were caught in the swirl of activity, and people in general took sides. Mrs. Annie Ruth Locklear Revels of Greensboro, N.C. best expressed the feeling of those who

Top. Historic Old Main. For many years this building was the focal point of Lumbee educational activities.

Center. The burning of Old Main, March 18, 1973.

Bottom. Standing silent in the wake of its destruction, Old Main, once restored, will house an Indian museum and cultural center, and the Department of American Indian Studies.

—Photos by Elmer Hunt

wanted to save Old Main in a poem and again in a letter. In her letter Mrs. Revels wrote,

> For many years the Lumbee Indians paid taxes, but had no schools. So I feel that we were done no great service when we were finally given a segragated institution, our first building costing a mere $75,000. Regardless of who paid for Old Main it belongs to the Lumbee Indians and all others who love it and would like to see it preserved. There is more than one way to own a thing. Some of the most precious things were not bought and paid for with money. Old Main belongs to me. I do not want to see it destroyed.

Those who did favor its destruction were motivated by practicality, not malice. Neither side had a monopoly on truth.

In the weeks that followed, the controversy intensified. Commissioner Brantly Blue appeared at a rally on February 4, 1972, and made an impassioned speech in which he said the real issue was Indian identity. He chided some Lumbees for not taking a bold stand. During this period several national Indian figures spoke out on the Old Main issue. Lewis R. Bruce, then Commissioner of the Bureau of Indian Affairs, said, "Old Main is a monument to the Indian people throughout this country." Leo Vacu, executive director of the National Congress of American Indians that year, wrote that "Indians everywhere have an interest in the Old Main Building at Pembroke State University." A figure who became increasingly important in the "Save-Old Main" movement was Janie Maynor Locklear. Not only was she outspoken and dedicated, she provided much of the leadership for the effort and eventually became executive-secretary of the "Old Main Commission," giving a sense of continuity to the entire movement. However, these were only a few of the voices, some great and some small, who expressed themselves on Old Main.

Old Main was burned, on a windy Sunday in March, against a background of both Tuscarora activity, and agitation over the building's future. The fire was discovered around 5:00 a.m. The fire department responded to the call, and when the men left they believed they had extinguished the blaze. As the Indians went to church, no trace of fire or smoke could be seen. But, following the

Sunday services, as the Indians returned to their homes, they saw Old Main consumed with flames that reached high into the heavens. The light wood timbers within the brick structure burned fiercely. As fire fighters struggled to save Old Main, Mrs. Janie Maynor Locklear walked around the building, thinking of her parents and other Indians in the first Normal graduating class in 1928. "Who could have done such a despicable thing!" she thought.

In the twilight of the evening, Governor Jim Holshouser, North Carolina's first Republican governor since 1901, arrived on the Pembroke University campus. In the glow of the dying fire, he spoke to a gathering of Indian people in front of Old Main. He promised action, and later offered a $5,000 reward for information leading to the arrest of the arsonist or arsonists. A few months later, he appointed an advisory board to study the possibilities of restoring the historic building. With $100,000 made available for the study, a commission was appointed, with John R. Jones as chairman. While the governor's role might be called "good politics," he was without question responding to the wishes of a majority of the Indian people.

In the Lumbee community, people still ask the question, "Who burned Old Main?" Sim Oxendine, chief of the Pembroke Fire Department, reported that the floors were soaked with oil. Months later, the odor of oil was still present. One Indian says concerning the arson:

> Some say it was White citizens,
> Some say it was an inside job,
> Others say it was the Tuscaroras,
> Some say it was PSU students,
> Still others say it was AIM.
> Who did it, it is done,
> Like the reward for the body of Henry Berry Lowry,
> The reward for the burning of Old Main will probably
> never be collected.

Since the fire, Pembroke State University has acquired additional land and is building its auditorium there. Plans have been drawn for the restoration of Old Main, with considerable contribution and activity from the community. At the start of 1974, the future of the historic building seems bright. If current plans are made effective, Old Main will house the American Indian Studies Department and a cultural center, including a regional Indian Museum. Those who fought to save the building say the outcome is sufficient reward for their efforts. Interestingly, the Old Main controversy and the "Tuscarora" movement seem to have produced comparable results. Both issues made the Indian people more aware of their Indianness, both got them more involved, and both caused public officials to be more responsive.

Although the Tuscarora movement retains a measure of vitality, it has become fragmented due to disagreements concerning tactics and religion. One former leader accepted a job offered by the governor and now works for change through the establishment; in his opinion the time for militancy has passed. But a more difficult problem for the Tuscaroras has been the question of Christianity. A few would abandon it in favor of a Native American religion, but others say they can't put down a faith they've known all their lives. Also, more and more the idea circulates among this faction that being Indian is not just a matter of blood, that it involves your lifestyle and your self-image. Until the Tuscaroras reconcile their internal differences, the direction in which their movement will go in the future is uncertain.

TODAY AND TOMORROW

It is usually the dramatic episode that demands the attention of history, and such has been the case with the Lumbees, but there is another side to the picture of the Indians who live in Robeson County. They are hard workers and basically a peaceful people. In rather undramatic fashion their constructive achievements have multiplied since the start of the seventies; the outlook for a continuation of this trend is favorable.

One of the more notable achievements of recent times was the opening on December 22, 1971, of the first Indian-owned bank in the United States. Lumbee Bank was chartered with more than six hundred stockholders, of which more than eighty percent were Lumbee Indians. With their share of the stock, the Lumbees constitute a majority of the board of directors. In 1973, the bank moved into a new, modern building located in Village Center, a shopping complex that is also Indian-owned. The total assets of the bank in 1974 were $5 million and growing. Serving all people in the area, the bank has brought new economic growth and new opportunities to the Indian people. However, the bank's business is not limited to Robeson County or North Carolina. Many corporations, and people of all races throughout the country, do business with this Indian financial institution. They know their investment is secure and they know they are helping a people who want to gain economic self-sufficiency. The opening of Lumbee Bank also made other banks in the area more considerate of their Indian customers. Competition can apparently change attitudes.

Another significant development has been the founding of a new newspaper, the *Carolina Indian Voice*. Although Pembroke has had several newspapers during the past forty years, none really succeeded. Two of the earliest were the *Odeka* and the *Pembroke Progress*, both of which used mainly voluntary help and concentrated on local news. In the 1960's a newspaper called *The Lumbee* was founded. During that period racial issues got many of the headlines and *The Lumbee* pressed hard for change in Robeson County. Unfortunately, many of its positions on issues were unpopular or controversial and the paper found it difficult to secure advertising. As a result, it finally went out of business, with the stockholders losing their investment of $30,000. The *Carolina Indian Voice* has a young, dynamic Lumbee editor. Bruce Barton's policy has been to make the newspaper into an instrument of progress for the Indian community. Speaking of his objectives, Barton said:

> We have named the organ the *Carolina Indian Voice* because we are Indians living in this country. We hope. . . to turn discrimination and poverty and other related ills inside out by honest, objective reporting of happenings in Robeson County. We are proud of our Indianness but are not close-minded to the friendship of whites, blacks, or Indians of other areas. We feel cooperation is the key to growth.

The newspaper has given the Lumbees their own independent source of news and a forum for self-expression.

When compared with other Indian tribes throughout the country, the Lumbees rate at the top of the scale politically, socially, and economically. Few, if any tribes can point to as much political involvement on the local, state, and national levels as the Lumbees, nor to as many college graduates, or as many economically independent Indian citizens. The Lumbees, despite the many problems of the past and present, know that they are relatively fortunate, and credit much of their success to their having never been wards of the government, as well as to their fertile, well-watered fields, which have given them an economic base seldom found among other tribes. The accuracy of this view is reflected in the comments of many Indians from other parts of the nation who have visited Lumbee country. Raymond Baines, a Tlingt Indian from Alaska, said, "The Lumbees are well ahead of any tribe I know." Homer Noley, a Choctaw, noted that "It appears the Lumbees have made much progress as a result of not being tied to the federal government." Robert Pinezaddleby of the Kiowa nation, said, "I will go back to Oklahoma and tell my people how well the Lumbees are doing." Gerald One Feather, a Sioux Indian from South Dakota, described the Lumbees as "more fortunate than most Indians." In short, most visitors are favorably impressed with the land, the people, and their accomplishments.

CONCLUSIONS

At the "First Convocation of American Indian Scholars," held in March, 1970 at Princeton University by the American Indian Historical Society, the question was asked, "How do Lumbee Indians know they are Indian?" On the following day of the Convocation, the well known novelist and scholar, N. Scott Momaday, a Kiowa Indian, said, "In one of the discussions yesterday, the question 'What is an American Indian?' was raised. The answer of course is that an Indian is an idea which a given man has of himself. And it is a moral idea, for it accounts for the way in which he reacts to other men and to the world in general. And that idea, in order to be realized completely, has to be expressed." Lumbee history, taken in total, has been an expression of the people's courage, their determination, their dreams, and their Indianness. Viewing the history of these people, it is an incontrovertible fact, moreover, that the Lumbees were recognized as Indians, were treated as Indians, were subjected to the same outrages as were all other Indians, and to this day conduct themselves as members of America's first people. Perhaps the secret of their success may be found in the same ideology expressed by their brothers living three thousand miles across the continent, the Cahuillas, who have always said, "If you let 'em do it to you, they will do it."

The road from obscurity and degradation has not been an easy one for the Lumbee Indians. The problems of origin, discrimination, and exploitation permeate their past. The problems of today plead for attention and demand answers. But the experiences of their history have done a great deal to shape the character of the people. If adversity produces an "inner strength," as some have suggested, then the Lumbees have acquired a great deal of that quality. The question now is, what is to come? Fittingly, a young Lumbee of the present generation said it best. "We can make the future whatever we want. When I look around and see what my people have overcome and are now doing, I'm proud to be a Lumbee."

Selected Bibliography

1. Manuscripts and Public Records

Bellamy, John D. "Remarks in the House of Representatives." North Carolina Collection, University of North Carolina—Chapel Hill.

"Freedmen's Bureau Records." Record Group 393, National Archives, Washington, D. C.

Gorman, John C. "Henry Berry Lowry Paper." North Carolina Division of Archives and History, Raleigh, N. C.

"Henry Berry Lowry Papers." North Carolina Division of Archives and History, Raleigh, N. C.

Lindquist, Gustarvis E. E. "The Lost Colony of Roanoke Today." North Carolina Collection, University of North Carolina—Chapel Hill.

McLean, Angus W. "Historical Sketch of the Indians of Robeson County." McLean Collection, Robeson County Public Library, Lumberton, N. C.

Moore, John W. (ed.). *Roster of North Carolina Troops in the War between the States.* 4 vols., Raleigh: State of North Carolina, 1882.

Muster Rolls of the Soldiers of the War of 1812: Detached from the Militia of North Carolina, In 1812 and 1814. Winston-Salem, 1926.

North Carolina. *Constitution of 1835.*

North Carolina. *Constitution of 1868.*

North Carolina. *Constitution of 1875.*

North Carolina. *Public Laws.*

North Carolina. *Reports of the Supreme Court.*

Roster of Soldiers from North Carolina in the American Revolution. Durham: North Carolina Daughters of the American Revolution, 1932.

Saunders, William L. (ed.) *The Colonial Records of North Carolina.* 10 vols., Raleigh: State of North Carolina, 1886-1890.

Swanton, John R. *Siouan Indians of the Lumber River.* House of Representatives Report No. 1752, Seventy-Third Congress, Second Session, 1934.

U. S. Bureau of the Census. *Eighth Census of the United States,* 1860.

U. S. Bureau of the Census. *U. S. Census of Population: 1970: North Carolina.*

The War of the Rebellion: A Compilation of the Official Records of the Union and Confederate Armies, 128 vols., Washington: Government Printing Office, 1880-1901.

Wishart, Colonel Francis. *Diary.* North Carolina Collection, University of North Carolina—Chapel Hill.

2. Interviews

Mr. and Mrs. Albert Bell. Sept. 5, 1971. Clinton, N. C.

Mr. Brantly Blue (Indian Claims Commissioner). July 24, 1971. Washington, D.C.

Mr. James K. Brayboy. Oct. 8, 1971. McColl, S. C.

Mr. Dolphus Brewington. Sept. 7, 1971. Clinton, N. C.

Mr. John David Brewington. July 21, 1973. Pembroke, N. C.

Mr. Colon Brooks. Sept. 2, 1969. Pembroke, N. C.

Miss Rosetta Brooks. Sept. 2, 1969. Pembroke, N. C.

Mr. Clement Bullard. July 22, 1969. Pembroke, N. C.

Judge Early Bullard. July 22, 1969. Pembroke, N. C.

Mr. Rand Bullard. July 18, 1969. Maxton, N. C.

Mrs. Amanda Carter. Oct. 15, 1971. Baltimore, Md.

Mr. John L. Carter, July 15, 1971. Pembroke, N. C.

Mrs. Rose Sampson Carter. Aug. 3, 1969. Pembroke, N. C.

Mr. Dannie Chavis. July 19, 1971. Pembroke, N. C.
Mr. James E. (Jim) Chavis. July 27, 1971; Aug. 19, 1971. Pembroke, N. C.
Mr. Oscar Chavis. Oct. 8, 1971. Lumberton, N. C.
Mrs. Willie C. Chavis. Aug. 27, 1971. Pembroke, N. C.
Mr. Danford Dial. Sept. 3, 1971. Pembroke, N. C.
Mr. Elisha Dial. July 26, 1971. Raeford, N. C.
Mr. Herman Dial (Robeson County Commissioner). April 16, 1974. Pembroke, N. C.
Rev. James Dial. Sept. 23, 1971. Baltimore, Md.
Mrs. N. H. Dial. Aug. 26, 1969. Pembroke, N. C.
Mr. Tommy Dial and others (Lumbee Regional Development Assoc. Convention).
     July 24, 1971. Wrightsville Beach, N. C.
Mr. John Godwin. May 30, 1969. Pembroke, N. C.
Mr. Charles Hunt. Sept. 23, 1971. Baltimore, Md.
Mrs. Mary Lowry Jacobs. July 26, 1969. Pembroke, N. C.
Mr. Miles S. Jones, Sr. Aug. 5, 1969. Pembroke, N. C.
Mr. Willoughby Jones. Aug. 28, 1969. Pembroke, N. C.
Mr. and Mrs. A. A. Lockee. Sept. 21, 1971. Pembroke, N. C.
Mr. Bobby Dean Locklear (Robeson County Commissioner). April 16, 1974. Red
     Springs, N. C.
Rev. C. E. Locklear. July 22, 1969; Aug. 28, 1969. Pembroke, N. C.
Mr. Fuller Locklear. Aug. 16, 1971. Pembroke, N. C.
Mr. Gaston Locklear. July 22, 1969. Pembroke, N. C.
Mr. Herbert Locklear. Sept. 23, 1971. Baltimore, Md.
Mr. James Allen Locklear. Aug. 3, 1969. Maxton, N. C.
Mrs. Nancy Chavis Locklear. Aug. 2, 1969. Maxton, N. C.
Mr. Person Locklear. Aug. 28, 1969. Red Springs, N. C.
Mrs. Willie Locklear. Sept. 3, 1971. Pembroke, N. C.
Rev. Harry Long (Creek Indian). Oct. 25, 1970. Oklahoma City, Okla.
Mrs. Anna Lowry. July 14, 1971. Pembroke, N. C.
Mr. Claude Lowry. Aug. 4, 1969. Pembroke, N. C.
Rev. D. F. Lowry. July 30, 1969; August 1, 1969; Oct. 4, 1969. Pembroke, N. C.
Mr. Daniel E. Lowry. Aug. 27, 1971; Sept. 8, 1971. Lumberton, N. C.
Mr. Lloyd Lowry. July 20, 1970. Pembroke, N. C.
Rev. Robert Mangum. Sept. 3, 1971. Pembroke, N. C.
Rev. Dawley Maynor. Aug. 27, 1971. Pembroke, N. C.
Mrs. C. H. Moore. Aug. 3, 1969. Maxton, N. C.
Mr. James Moore. Aug. 3, 1969. Maxton, N. C.
Mr. Charlie W. Oxendine. July 19, 1969; Sept. 7, 1971. Pembroke, N. C.
Mr. Clifton Oxendine, Professor Emeritus. July 30, 1969. Pembroke State University.
Mr. J. C. Oxendine. March 21, 1974. Pembroke, N. C.
Mr. Simeon (Sim) Oxendine. Sept., 1973. Pembroke, N. C.
Mr. George Ransom. July 26, 1969. Pembroke, N. C.
Charlie Rose, United States Congressman, 7th Congressional District, North Caro-
     lina, July, 1972.
Mrs. Nancy Lowry Revels. July 27, 1971. Pembroke, N. C.
Mrs. Betty Rogers. July 26, 1971. Raeford, N. C.
Mr. Mabe Sampson. May 30, 1969. Pembroke, N. C.
Mr. Joe Sando. July, 1971. Albuquerque, New Mexico.
Ms. Helen Scheirbeck. Fall, 1973. Pembroke, N. C.
Dr. Gerald M. Sider. Aug. 19, 1971. New York, N. Y.

3. Books and Pamphlets
Amanullah, Mohammod. *The Lumbee Indians: Patterns of Adjustment.* Washing-
     ton: Government Printing Office, 1969.
Barrett, John G. *Sherman's March Through the Carolinas.* Chapel Hill: University
     of North Carolina Press, 1956.

Barton, Lewis R. *The Most Ironic Story in American History.* Charlotte, N. C.: Associated Printing Corporation, 1967.

Berry, Brewton. *Almost White.* New York: The Macmillan Company, 1963.

Blu, Karen J. "Lumbee," in *Handbook of North American Indians.* William C. Sturtevant, Gen. Ed., Washington, D. C.: Smithsonian Press.

Brewington, C. D. *The Five Civilized Indian Tribes of Eastern North Carolina.* Clinton, N. C.: Bass Publishing Company, n.d.

Cummings, William P. *The Southeast in Early Maps.* Chapel Hill: University of North Carolina Press, 1958.

Deloria, Vine, Jr. *Custer Died for Your Sins, An Indian Manifesto.* New York: Macmillan and Company, 1969.

Eaton, Joseph. *Exploring Tomorrow's Agriculture.* New York: Harper Brothers, 1943.

Evans, W. McKee. *Ballots and Fence Rails: Reconstruction on the Lower Cape Fear.* Chapel Hill: University of North Carolina Press, 1966.

_____. *To Die Game: The Story of the Lowry Band, Indian Guerrillas of Reconstruction.* Baton Rouge: Louisiana State University Press, 1971.

Farris, James J. "The Lowrie Gang: An Episode in the History of Robeson County, N. C., 1865-1874," in *Historical Papers Published by the Trinity College Historical Society.* Series XV, Durham: Duke University Press, 55-93.

Ferguson, Robert, and Jesse Burt. *Indians of the Southeast: Then and Now.* Nashville: Abingdon Press, 1973.

Fitch, William Edward. *The First Founders in America, with Facts to Prove That Sir Walter Raleigh's Lost Colony Was Not Lost.* New York, The New York Society of the Order of the Founders and Patriots of America, 1913.

Green, Paul E. *The Last of the Lowries.* New York: Samuel French, Inc., 1922.

Gregg, Alexander. *History of the Old Cheraws.* New York: Richardson and Company, 1867.

Hamilton, Joseph G. D. *Reconstruction in North Carolina.* New York: Columbia University Press, 1914.

Hawks, Francis L. *History of North Carolina: From 1663 to 1729.* 2 vols., Fayetteville, N. C.: E. J. Hale & Son, 1858.

Hudson, Charles M. *The Catawba Nation.* Athens: University of Georgia Press, 1970.

Indian Voices: The First Convocation of American Indian Scholars. San Francisco: The Indian Historian Press, 1970.

Johnson, Guion G. *Ante-Bellum North Carolina: A Social History.* Chapel Hill: University of North Carolina Press, 1937.

Lawrence, Robert C. *The State of Robeson.* Lumberton, North Carolina: J. J. Little and Ives Company, 1939.

Lawson, John. *A New Voyage to Carolina.* Ed. and annotated by Hugh T. Lefler. Chapel Hill: University of North Carolina Press, 1967.

Lee, E. Lawrence. *Indian Wars in North Carolina 1663-1763.* Raleigh: State Department of Archives and History, 1968.

The Lower Cape Fear in Colonial Days. Chapel Hill: University of North Carolina Press, 1965.

Lefler, Hugh T. and Albert Ray Newsome. *North Carolina: The History of a Southern State.* 3rd ed., Chapel Hill: University of North Carolina Press, 1973.

Lowrey, Clarence E. *The Invasion of America.* Lumberton, N. C.: Private Publication, 1960.

_____. *The Lumbee Indians of North Carolina.* Lumberton, N. C.: Private Publication, 1960.

Lucas, John Paul, Jr., and Bailey T. Groome. *The King of Scuffletown: A Croatan Romance.* Richmond: Garrett and Massie, Inc., 1940.

McLean, Angus W., and others. *Lumber River Scots and Their Descendants.* Richmond: William Byrd Press, 1942.

McMillan, Hamilton. *Sir Walter Raleigh's Lost Colony.* Raleigh: Edwards and Broughton Company, 1888.

McPherson, O. M. (compiler). *Indians of North Carolina.* Washington: Government Printing Office, 1915.

Meyer, Duane. *The Highland Scots of North Carolina, 1732-1776.* Chapel Hill: University of North Carolina Press, 1961.

Milling, Chapman J. *Red Carolinians.* Chapel Hill: University of North Carolina Press, 1940.

Mooney, James, "Croatan," in *Handbook of Indians North of Mexico.* Bulletin 30, Washington: Bureau of American Ethnology, 1907.

Morison, Samuel Eliot. *The European Discovery of America: The Northern Voyages A. D. 500-1600.* New York: Oxford University Press, 1971.

Morgan, Ernest W. "A Racial Comparison of Education in Robeson County, North Carolina." M. A. thesis, University of North Carolina—Chapel Hill, 1940.

Norment, Mary C. *The Lowrie History.* Wilmington: Daily Journal Printer, 1875.

Oates, John A. *The Story of Fayetteville and the Upper Cape Fear.* Charlotte: The Dowd Press, Inc., 1950.

Owen, Guy. *Journey for Joedel.* New York: Crown Publishers Inc., 1970.

Rights, Douglas L. *The American Indian in North Carolina.* 2nd ed., Winston-Salem: John F. Blair, Publisher, 1957.

South, Stanley A. *Indians in North Carolina.* Raleigh: State Department of Archives and History, 1965.

Sprunt, James. *Chronicles of the Cape Fear River, 1660-1916.* Raleigh Edwards and Broughton Company, 1914.

Swanton, John R. *Probable Identity of the "Croatan" Indians.* Bulletin, Washington: Office of Indian Affairs, 1933.

Townsend, George A. (compiler). *The Swamp Outlaws.* New York: Robert M. Dewitt, 1872.

4. Articles

Barton, Lewis R. "Henry Berry Lowry, Lumbee Guerrilla Warrior of Reconstruction Days," *Indian Voice,* Vol. 1, No. 7 (September 14, 1972).

—————. "Me-Told Tales Along the Lumbee," *North Carolina Folklore,* Vol. XIX, No. 4 (November, 1971), 173-176.

Chavers, Dean. "The Lumbee Story, Part I—Origin of the Tribe," *Indian Voice,* Vol. 1, No. 10 (1971-72), 11-12, 24.

Cox, William Norment. "The Scuffletown Outlaws," *Southwest Review,* 1926.

Craven, Charles. "The Robeson County Indian Uprising Against the KKK," *The South Atlantic Quarterly,* Vol. LVII (1958), 433-442.

Dart, A. D. "Raleigh's Lost Colony," *The Southern Workman* (August, 1913).

Dial, Adolph L. "The Lumbee Indians: Still a Lost Colony?" *New World Outlook* (May, 1972), 19-22.

Dial, Adolph L. and David K. Eliades. "The Lumbee Indians of North Carolina and Pembroke State University," *The Indian Historian.* (Winter, 1971), 20-24.

Dunlap, A. R. and C. A. Weslager. "Trends in the Naming of Tri-Racial Mix-Blood Groups in the Eastern United States," *American Speech,* Vol. 22, No. 2, 81-87.

Dunnagan, Claude. "Henry Lowry's Private Six-Year War Against the South," *Male,* Vol. 11, No. 7 (July, 1971).

Edgerton, John. "Six Districts, Three Races and More Things," *Southern Education Report* (December, 1968), 4-10.

Gaillard, Frye. "Desegregation Denies Justice to Lumbee Indians," *The Indian Historian,* Vol. 4, No. 3 (Fall, 1971), 17-22, 43.

Gilbert, William Harlan, Jr., "Memorandum Concerning the Characteristics of the Larger Mixed Blood Racial Islands of the Eastern United States," *Social Forces,* Vol. 24, No. 4 (May, 1946).

Greensboro *Daily News.* "Indians of North Carolina Series—The Lumbees." (January 17-20), 1971.

Harper, Roland M. "The Most Prolific People in the United States," *Eugenics News,* Vol. 23, No. 2 (March-April, 1938).

_____. "A Statistical Study of the Croatans," *Rural Sociology,* Vol. 2, No. 4 (December, 1937), 444-456.

Haynes, William. "Down the Old Lumbee," *Field and Stream.* (May, 1918), 5-7, 48.

Johnson, Guy B. "Personality in a White-Indian-Negro Community," *American Sociological Review,* Vol. 4, No. 4 (1939), 516-523.

Lowry, D. F. "No Mystery," *The State,* Vol. 20, No. 29 (December 20, 1952), p. 24.

McKay, Arnold A. "Nobody Knows Anything about the Croatans," *The State.* (February 24, 1934).

Melton, Francis J. "Croatans: The Lost Colony of America," *Mid-Continent Magazine,* Vol. 6 (July, 1885).

Oxendine, Clifton. "Pembroke State College for Indians," *North Carolina Historical Review,* XXII (January, 1945), 22-33.

Parsons, Elsie C. "Folklore of the Cherokees of Robeson County, N. C.," *Journal of American Folklore,* Vol. 32, No. 125 (July-September, 1919), 384-393.

Peck, John Gregory. "Indians and Their Education in Baltimore." ERIC Document Reproduction Service, Bethesda, Maryland, 1971.

_____. "Robeson County, North Carolina." ERIC Document Reproduction Service, Bethesda, Maryland, 1971.

Purcell, J. E., Jr. "The Croatan Indians," *Davidson College Magazine,* Vol. 21, No. 6 (1905), 263-265.

Sturtevant, William C. and Samuel Stanley, "Indian Communities in the Eastern States," *The Indian Historian,* Vol. 1, No. 3 (1968), 15-19.

Weeks, Stephen B. "The Lost Colony of Roanoke: Its Fate and Survival," *Papers* of the American Historical Association, Vol. 5, Part 4 (1891), 107-146.

5. Newspapers
Akwesasne Notes (Rooseveltown, New York).
Carolina Indian Voice (Pembroke, N. C.).
Charlotte Observer.
Daily News (Greensboro).
Fayetteville Observer.
Lumbee (Pembroke, N. C.).
Lumberton Post.
News and Observer (Raleigh, N. C.).
Robesonian (Lumberton, N. C.).
Wassaja (San Francisco, Ca.).

6. Unpublished Studies
Barnes, Bahnson N. "A History of the Robeson County School System." M. A. thesis, University of North Carolina—Chapel Hill, 1931.

Beckwith, Evalina G. "A Study of the Physical Equipment and Teaching Personnel of the Indian Schools of Robeson County." M. A. thesis, University of North Carolina—Chapel Hill, 1950.

Blu, Karen J. "We People: Understanding Lumbee Indian Identity in a Tri-Racial Situation." Ph. D. dissertation, University of Chicago, 1972.

Hancock, Earnest D. "A Sociological Study of the Tri-Racial Community in Robeson County, N. C." M. A. thesis, University of North Carolina—Chapel Hill, 1935.

Makofsky, Abraham. "Tradition and Change in the Lumbee Indian Community of Baltimore." Ph. D. dissertation, Catholic University, 1971.

Oxendine, Clifton. "A Social and Economic History of the Indians of Robeson County, North Carolina." M. A. thesis, George Peabody College, 1934.

Sider, Gerald M. "The Political History of the Lumbee Indians of Robeson County, North Carolina." Ph. D. dissertation, New School for Social Research, 1971.

Thompson, Vernon Ray. "A History of the Education of the Lumbee Indians of Robeson County, North Carolina, 1885-1970." Ph. D. dissertation, University of Miami, 1973.

_____. "A Study of the Indian Schools of Robeson County, North Carolina." M. A. thesis, Ohio State University, 1951.

Appendices

APPENDIX A

List of the "Lost Colonists"

MEN

John White
Roger Baily
Ananias Dare
Christopher Cooper
Thomas Stevens
John Sampson
Dionys Harvie
Roger Prat
George Howe
Simon Fernando
Nicholas Johnson
Thomas Warner
Anthony Cage
William Willes
William Brown
Michael Myllet
Thomas Smith
Richard Kemme
Thomas Harris
Richard Taverner
William Clement
Robert Little
Hugh Tayler
William Berde
Richard Wildye
Lewes Wotton
Michael Bishop
Henry Browne
Henry Rufotte
Richard Tomkins
Henry Dorrell
John Jones
John Brooks
Cutbert White
John Bright
Clement Taylor
William Sole
John Cotsmuir
Humphrey Newton
William Waters
Richard Arthur
John Chapman
James Lasie

Thomas Colman
Thomas Gramme, or Graham, Graeme
Mark Bennet
John Gibbes
John Stilman
John Earnest
Henry Johnson
John Starte
Richard Darige
William Lucas
Arnold Archard
William Nichols
Thomas Phevens
John Borden
Charles Florrie
Henry Mylton
Henry Paine
Thomas Harris
Thomas Scot
Peter Little
John Wyles
Bryan Wyles
Robert Wilkinson
John Tydway
Ambrose Viccars
Edmund English
Thomas Topan
Henry Berry
Richard Berry
John Spendlove
John Hemmington
Thomas Butler
Edward Powell
John Burdon
James Hynde
Thomas Ellis
John Wright
William Dutton
Maurice Allen
Hugh Pattenson
Martin Sutton
John Farre
John Bridger

John Cheven	Griffin Jones
Thomas Hewett	Richard Shabedge
George Martin	

WOMEN

Eleanor Dare	Alice Charman
Margery Harvie	Emma Merimoth
Agnes Wood	_____ Colman
Winnifred Powell	Margaret Lawrence
Joyce Archard	Joan Warren
Jane Jones	Jane Mannering
Elizabeth Glane	Rose Payne
Jane Pierce	Elizabeth Viccars
Andry Tappan	

BOYS AND CHILDREN

John Sampson	Thomas Smart
Robert Ellis	George Howe
Ambrose Viccas	John Prat
Thomas Archard	William Wythers
Thomas Humphrey	

CHILDREN BORN IN VIRGINIA

| Virginia Dare | _____ Harvie |

APPENDIX B

NOTABLE LEGISLATION IN LUMBEE HISTORY

AN ACT To provide for separate schools for Croatan Indians in Robeson County.

Whereas the Indians now living in Robeson County claim to be descendants of a friendly tribe who once resided in eastern North Carolina on the Roanoke River, known as the Croatan Indians; therefore,

The General Assembly of North Carolina do enact:

SECTION 1. That the said Indians and their descendants shall hereafter be designated and known as the Croatan Indians.

SECTION 2. That said Indians and their descendants shall have separate schools for their children, school committees of their own race and color, and shall be allowed to select teachers of their own choice, subject to the same rules and regulations as are applicable to all teachers in the general school law.

SECTION 3. It shall be the duty of the county board of education to see that this act is carried into effect, and shall for that purpose have the census of all the children of said Indians and their descendants between the ages of six and twenty-one taken, and proceed to establish such suitable school districts as shall be necessary for their convenience, and take all such other and further steps as may be necessary for the purpose of carrying this act into effect without delay.

SECTION 4. The treasurer and other proper authorities, whose duties it is to collect, keep, and apportion to the school fund, shall procure from the county board of education the number of children in said county between the ages of six and twenty-one, belonging to said Indian race, and shall set apart and keep separate their pro rata share of said school funds, which shall be paid out upon the same rules in every respect as are provided in general school law; Provided, That where any children, descendants of Indians as aforesaid, shall reside in any district in which there are no schools, as provided in this chapter, the same shall have the right to attend any of the public schools in said county for their race, and shall be allowed to draw their share of public school fund upon the certificate of the school committee in the district in which they reside, stating that they have thus removed and are entitled to attend public schools.

SECTION 5. The general school law shall be applicable in all respects to this chapter, where the same is not repugnant to or inconsistent with this act. This act shall only apply to Robeson County. All laws and clauses of law in conflict with this act are hereby repealed.

SECTION 6. That this act shall be in force from and after its ratification.

(In the General Assembly read three times and ratified this the 10th day of February, A. D. 1885.)

[Laws of North Carolina, 1885, chapter 51.]

AN ACT To establish a normal school in the county of Robeson.

The General Assembly of North Carolina do enact:

SECTION 1. That W. L. Moore, James Oxendine, James Dial, Preston Locklear, and others who may be associated with them, and their successors, are hereby constituted a body politic and corporate, for educational purposes, in the county of Robeson, under the name and style of the trustees of the Croatan Normal School, and by that name may have perpetual succession, may sue and be sued, plead and be impleaded, contract and be contracted with, to have and to hold school property, including buildings, lands, and all appurtenances thereto, situated in the county of Robeson, at any place in said county to be selected by the trustees herein named, provided such place shall be located between Bear Swamp and Lumber River in said county; to acquire by purchase, donation, or otherwise, real and personal property for the purpose of establishing and maintaining a school of high grade for teachers of the Croatan race in North Carolina.

SECTION 2. That the trustees at their organization shall elect one of their own number president of the board of trustees, whose duties shall be such as develops upon such officers in similar cases, or such as shall hereafter be defined by said trustees.

SECTION 3. That said trustees shall have full power to rent, lease, mortgage or sell any real or personal property for the purpose of maintaining said school, discharging indebtedness, or reinvesting the proceeds for a like purpose: Provided, That the liabilities of said trustees shall affect only the property owned by said trustees for educational purposes and shall not affect the private credit of said trustees.

SECTION 4. That the trustees whose names are mentioned in the first section of this act shall have the power to select three additional trustees from the Croatan race in such manner as they may determine.

SECTION 5. That said trustees shall have full power and authority to employ a teacher or teachers in said normal school under such regulations as the said trustees may determine.

SECTION 6. That said board of trustees shall have full power to fill all vacancies by death, removal, or otherwise in said board: Provided, a majority vote of all the trustees shall be necessary to a choice.

SECTION 7. That the sum of five hundred dollars is hereby appropriated to the support of said school annually for two years, and no longer, commencing with the first day of January, one thousand eight hundred and eighty-eight, said sum to be paid out of the general educational fund: Provided, That said sum thus appropriated shall be expended for the payment of services rendered for teaching and for no other purpose; said sum to be paid in semiannual payments upon warrants drawn by State superintendent of public instruction upon receipt by said superintendent of report of trustees of said school showing the number of teachers employed, the amount paid to teacher, the number of students in attendance during the term of six months next preceding the first day of July, one thousand eight hundred and eighty-eight, first day of January, one thousand eight hundred and eighty-nine, first day of July, one thousand eight hundred and eighty-nine, and first day of January, one thousand eight hundred and ninety.

SECTION 8. That all property, real and personal, acquired by purchase, donation, or otherwise, as long as it is used for educational purposes, shall be exempt from taxation, whether on the part of the State or county.

SECTION 9. That no person shall sell any spirituous liquors within two miles of the location of said school, and any person violating this section shall be guilty of a misdemeanor, and upon conviction shall be fined not less than ten dollars nor more than thirty dollars, or imprisoned not less than ten days nor more than thirty days, or both at the discretion of the court.

SECTION 10. Provided, That no person shall be admitted into said school as a student who has not attained the age of fifteen years; and that all those who shall enjoy the privileges of said school as students shall previously obligate (themselves) to teach the youth of the Croatan race for a stated period.

SECTION 11. That this act shall be in force from and after its ratification.

(In the General Assembly read three times, and ratified this 7th day of March, A. D. 1887.)

[Laws of North Carolina, chapter 400.]

AN ACT To empower the trustees of the Indian School of Robeson County to transfer title to property of said school by deed to State board of education, and to provide for the appointment of trustees for said school.

The General Assembly of North Carolina do enact:

SECTION 1. That in accordance with the recent action of the trustees, in meeting assembled, of the Croatan State normal school, known as the Indian Normal School of Robeson County, situated near Pembroke, North Carolina, said school being incorporated under Chapter Four hundred, Public Laws of One thousand eight hundred and eighty-seven, which action of the trustees of said school has been duly certified to by the president, C. R. Sampson, and the secretary, A. A. Locklear, the said trustees are hereby empowered to convey by deed to the State board of education the title to all property of said school, and the State board of education is hereby authorized to accept same.

SECTION 2. That the State board of education shall appoint seven members of the Indian race, formally known as Croatans, to be constituted the board of trustees of said school, as follows: Two members for the term of two years, two for the term of four years, and three for the term of six years; and, at the expiration of these terms, their successors shall be appointed by the State board of education for a term of six years.

SECTION 3. That the board of trustees of said Indian normal school Robeson County shall have the power to employ and discharge teachers, to prevent negroes from attending said school, and to exercise the usual functions of control and management of said school, their action being subject to the approval of the State board of education.

SECTION 4. That all laws and clauses of laws in conflict with this act are hereby repealed.

SECTION 5. This act shall be in force from and after its ratification.

(Ratified this the 8th day of March, A. D. 1911.)

[Public laws of North Carolina, session of 1911, chapter 168.]

AN ACT To change the name of the Indians in Robeson County and to provide for said Indians separate apartments in the state hospital.

The General Assembly of North Carolina do enact:

SECTION 1. That Chapter Fifty-one of the Public laws of North Carolina, session of eighteen hundred and eighty-five, be, and the same is hereby, amended by striking out the words "Croatan Indians" wherever the same occur in said chapter and inserting in lieu thereof the words "Indians of Robeson County."

SECTION 2. That in all laws enacted by the General Assembly of North Carolina relating to said Indians subsequent to the enactment of said Chapter Fifty-one of the Laws of Eighteen hundred and eighty-five, the words "Croatan Indians" be, and the same are hereby, stricken out and the words "Indians of Robeson County" inserted in lieu thereof.

SECTION 3. And that the said Indians residing in Robeson and adjoining counties which have heretofore been known as Croatan Indians, together with their descendants, shall hereafter be known and designated as "Indians of Robeson County," and by that name shall be entitled to all the rights and privileges conferred by any of the laws of North Carolina upon the Indians heretofore known as Croatan Indians.

SECTION 4. That the school situated near the town of Pembroke, in Robeson County, known as Croatan Indian Normal School, shall hereafter be known and designated as "The Indian Normal School of Robeson County," and in that name shall be entitled to all of the privileges and powers heretofore conferred by any law of the State of North Carolina or any laws hereafter enacted for the benefit of said school.

SECTION 5. That the board of directors for the State Hospital for the Insane at Raleigh are hereby authorized and directed to provide and set apart at said hospital, as soon after the passage of this act as practicable, suitable apartments and wards for the accommodation of any of said Indians of Robeson County who may be entitled under the laws relating to insane persons to be admitted to said hospital.

SECTION 6. That the sheriff, jailer, or other proper authorities of Robeson County shall provide in the common jail of Robeson County and in the Home for the Aged and Infirm of Robeson County separate cells, wards, or apartments for the said Indians of Robeson County, in all cases where it shall be necessary under the laws of this State to commit any of said Indians to said jail or County Home for the Aged and Infirm.

SECTION 7. That all laws and clauses of laws in conflict with this act are hereby repealed.

SECTION 8. That this act shall be in force from and after its ratification.

(Ratified this 8th day of March, A. D. 1911.)

[Public Laws of North Carolina, Session of 1911, Chapter 215.]

AN ACT To restore to the Indians residing in Robeson and adjoining counties their rightful and ancient name.

The General Assembly of North Carolina do enact:

SECTION 1. That Chapter Two hundred and fifteen of the Public Laws of North Carolina, session one thousand nine hundred and eleven, be, and the same is hereby, amended by striking out in the last line of said section one of the words "Indians of Robeson County," and inserting in lieu thereof the words "Cherokee Indians of Robeson County."

SECTION 2. That section two of said Chapter Two hundred and fifteen of the Public Laws of North Carolina, session one thousand nine hundred and eleven, be, and the same is hereby, amended by striking out the words "Indians of Robeson County," in the fifth line of said section two, and inserting in lieu thereof the words "Cherokee Indians of Robeson County."

SECTION 3. That said Chapter Two hundred and fifteen of the Public Laws of North Carolina, session one thousand nine hundred and eleven, be further amended by striking out the words "Indians of Robeson County," in line four of said section three, and inserting in lieu thereof the words "Cherokee Indians of Robeson County."

SECTION 4. That the Indians residing in Robeson and adjoining counties who have heretofore been known as "Croatan Indians" or "Indians of Robeson County," together with their descendants, shall hereafter be known and designated as "Cherokee Indians of Robeson County," and by that name shall be entitled to all the rights and privileges heretofore or hereafter conferred by any law or laws of the State of North Carolina upon the Indians heretofore known as the "Croatan Indians" or "Indians of Robeson County," including all such rights and privileges as have been conferred upon said Indians by Chapter Two hundred and fifteen of the Public Laws of North Carolina, session one thousand nine hundred and eleven.

SECTION 5. Neither this act nor any other act relating to said "Cherokee Indians of Robeson County" shall be construed so as to impose on said Indians any powers, privileges, rights, or immunities or any limitations on their power to contact, heretofore enacted with reference to the Eastern Band of Cherokee Indians, residing in Cherokee, Graham, Swain, Jackson, and other adjoining counties in North Carolina, or any other band of Cherokee Indians other than those now residing, or who have, since the Revolutionary War, resided in Robeson County, nor shall said "Cherokee Indians of Robeson County," as herein designated be subject to the limitations provided in section nine hundred and seventy-five and nine hundred and seventy-six of the revisal of one thousand nine hundred and five of North Carolina.

SECTION 6. That Chapter Two hundred and fifteen of the Public Law of North Carolina, session one thousand nine hundred and eleven, be further amended by striking out the words "Indian Normal School of Robeson County," in the third and fourth lines of said section four of said Chapter Two hundred and fifteen, and inserting in lieu thereof the words "Cherokee Indian Normal School of Robeson County."

SECTION 7. That all laws and clauses of laws in conflict with the provisions of this act are hereby repealed.

SECTION 8. That this act shall be in force and effect from and after its ratification.

(In the general assembly read three times and ratified this the 11th day of March, 1913.)

[Public Laws of North Carolina, Session of 1913, Chapter 123.]

AN ACT Relating to the Lumbee Indians of North Carolina.

Whereas many Indians now living in Robeson and adjoining counties are descendants of that once large and prosperous tribe which occupied the lands along the Lumbee River at the time of the earliest white settlements in that section; and

Whereas at the time of their first contacts wih the colonists, these Indians were a well-established and distinctive people living in European-type houses in settled towns, and communities, owning slaves and livestock, tilling the soil, and practicing many of the arts and crafts of European civilization; and

Whereas by reason of tribal legend, coupled with a distinctive appearance and manner of speech and the frequent recurrence among them of family names such as Oxendine, Locklear, Chavis, Drinkwater, Bullard, Lowery, Sampson, and others, also found on the roster of the earliest English settlements, these Indians may, with considerable show of reason, trace their origin to an admixture of colonial blood with certain coastal tribes of Indians; and

Whereas these people are naturally and understandably proud of their heritage, and desirous of establishing their social status and preserving their racial history: Now, therefore,

Be it enacted by the Senate and House of Representatives of the United States of America in Congress assembled, That the Indians now residing in Robeson and adjoining counties of North Carolina, originally found by the first white settlers on the Lumbee River in Robeson County, and claiming joint descent from remnants of early American colonists and certain tribes of Indians originally inhabiting the coastal regions of North Carolina, shall, from and after the ratification of this Act, be known and designated as Lumbee Indians of North Carolina and shall continue to enjoy all rights, privileges, and immunities enjoyed by them as citizens of the State of North Carolina and of the United States as they enjoyed before the enactment of this Act, and shall continue to be subject to all the obligations and duties of such citizens under the laws of the State of North Carolina and the United States. Nothing in this Act shall make such Indians eligible for any services performed by the United States for Indians because of their status as Indians, and none of the statutes of the United States which affect Indians because of their status as Indians shall be applicable to the Lumbee Indians.[1]

SECTION 2.   All laws and parts of laws in conflict with this Act are hereby repealed.

(Ratified this the 7th day of June, A. D. 1956.)

[Public Law 570, 84th Congress, Chapter 375, 2nd Session.]

1. A bill to amend the Lumbee Act by deleting the last sentence in Section 1 was under consideration by the United States Congress in 1974.

APPENDIX C

Lumbees Involved in National Indian Affairs

Brantly Blue, Indian Claims Commissioner.

Dr. Bobby Brayboy, Acting Chief, Physician Recruitment and Supportive Branch of the Indian Health Service.

Betty Jo Hunt, Assistant to the Council, Sub-Committee on Indian Affairs, United States House of Representatives; advisor on Indian affairs to the Presbyterian Church NSA and the Lutheran Church.

Linda Oxendine, Associate of the National Congress of American Indians and Coalition of Eastern Native Americans.

Lloyd Oxendine, Director of Native American Artists, New York.

Thomas Oxendine, Acting Director of the Office of Communication, Bureau of Indian Affairs.

Helen Maynor Scheirbeck, Director of Indian Education, Department of Health, Education, and Welfare.

W. J. Strickland, Co-Director of the Coalition of Eastern Native Americans.

Purnell Swett, Program Manager, Indian Education, Department of Health, Education, and Welfare.

APPENDIX D

Lumbees Serving in Elective Offices 1974

North Carolina House of Representatives
Henry Ward Oxendine

Robeson County Board of Commissioners
Herman Dial
Bobby Dean Locklear

Hoke County Board of Commissioners
James Hunt

Robeson County Board of Education
Harold Dial
Mrs. Ailene Holmes
Harry West Locklear
Harbert Moore
Simeon Oxendine

Lumberton City Council
Hilton Oxendine

Pembroke Town Council
Juddie Revels, Mayor
Lee Neville
Reggie Strickland
J. C. Thomas
Fairley Woodell

Lumberton Board of Education
Mrs. Zelma Locklear

Maxton Board of Education
Palmer Ray Bryant

Fairmont Board of Education
James A. Freeman

THE
Iroquois
AND THEIR
NEIGHBORS   Laurence M. Hauptman, *Series Editor*

This series presents a wide range of scholarship—archaeology, anthropology, history, public policy, sociology, women's studies—that focuses on the indigenous peoples of northeastern North America. The series encourages more awareness and a broader understanding of the Iroquois Indians—the Mohawk, Oneida, Onondaga, Cayuga, Seneca, and Tuscarora—and their Native American neighbors and provides a forum for scholars to elucidate the important contributions of the first Americans from prehistory to the present day.

Selected titles in the series include:

American Indian Environments: Ecological Issues in Native American History. Christopher Vecsey and Robert W. Venables, ed.

Apologies to the Iroquois. Edmund Wilson

Beyond the Covenant Chain: The Iroquois and Their Neighbors in Indian North America, 1600–1800. Daniel K. Richter and James H. Merrell, eds.

Conservatism Among the Iroquois at the Six Nations Reserve. Annemarie Anrod Shimony

An Ethnography of the Huron Indians, 1615–1649. Elisabeth Tooker

Evolution of the Onondaga Iroquois: Accommodating Change, 1500–1655. James W. Bradley

Fighting Tuscarora: The Autobiography of Chief Clinton Rickard. Barbara Graymont, ed.

The History and Culture of Iroquois Diplomacy: An Interdisciplinary Guide to the Treaties of the Six Nations and Their League. Francis Jennings, ed.

The Iroquois and the New Deal. Laurence M. Hauptman

The Iroquois Eagle Dance: An Offshoot of the Calumet Dance. William N. Fenton

The Iroquois in the American Revolution. Barbara Graymont

The Iroquois in the Civil War: From Battlefield to Reservation. Laurence M. Hauptman

Iroquois Land Claims. Christopher Vecsey and William A. Starna, eds.

Iroquois Medical Botany. James W. Herrick and Dean R. Snow

The Iroquois Struggle for Survival: World War II to Red Power. Laurence M. Hauptman

Joseph Brant, 1743–1807: Man of Two Worlds. Isabel Thompson Kelsay

King of the Delawares: Teedyuscung, 1700–1763. Anthony F. C. Wallace

The Mashpee Indians: Tribe on Trial. Jack Campisi

A Narrative of the Life of Mrs. Mary Jemison. James E. Seaver

The Oneida Land Claims: A Legal History. George C. Shattuck

Onondaga Iroquois Prehistory: A Study in Settlement Archaeology. James A. Tuck

Parker on the Iroquois. Arthur C. Parker; William N. Fenton, ed.

Skunny Wundy: Seneca Indian Tales. Arthur C. Parker

To Die Game: The Story of Lowry Band, Indian Guerillas of Reconstruction. William McKee Evans

Warrior in Two Camps: Ely S. Parker, Union General and Seneca Chief. William H. Armstrong